Stories of My Life

by: Sydell Weiner

(née Horowitz)

Stories of My Life

Disclaimer:

This memoir is a work of nonfiction. The events and experiences described in this book are based on the author's personal recollections and memories. Every effort has been made to provide an accurate account of these events as truthfully and faithfully as possible. Any inconsistencies are purely unintentional and are a result of the nature of memory.

Special Thanks to Phil Crandlemire
Typesetter, Designer, Layout Artist, and Editor

With love for all your tomorrows

Table of Contents

Chapter One - The Early Years

Chapter Two - Finding My Way

Chapter Three - Love and Loss

Chapter Four - Reflections

Chapter One

The Early Years

Where I Come From

November 1963

I come from latkes draining on my grandmother's stove
Her chicken soup simmering and stirring my soul

I'm from post-war migration to the suburbs of New York
"Little Boxes on the Hillside "like our Long Island home

I'm from three new dresses for the Jewish High Holidays
With new shoes, hats and gloves to match

I'm from that funny lawyer and his beautiful wife
Their steadfast courage when Illness struck home

I'm from early mother loss and pretending to be fine
A smiling cheerleader in love with the crowd

I'm from Yale School of Drama and NYU
Reinventing the classics and directing new plays

I'm from immigrant families, who paved the way
For my son the rabbi and daughter's successful career

I'm from strength to strength as I learned resilience
And behold the future in my grandchildren's eyes

Sarah Heartburn

My parents called me Sarah Bernhardt, which my father changed to Sarah Heartburn. I wore the title with pride because my parents paid attention to me when I was cute and funny. But there was something underneath that I had to keep hidden. I was highly sensitive.

It was more than just being emotional. I was moved by the oddest things, and my feelings were so intense. A beautiful melody or loving words would make me wild with joy. But if the tune turned dissonant or the words became harsh, I would suffer for days.

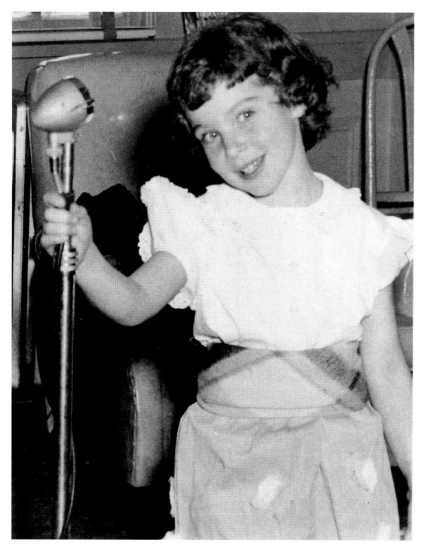

Sydell Horowitz, December 1951

My parents were both children of immigrants, raised during the Depression. The only way to get ahead in their world was to hold IN your feelings and do what you're told. I tried to comply and was often convincing. But I had too many feelings that I couldn't control.

I was particularly sensitive to the arts. In high school, while my friends hung out at the mall, I took the train to Manhattan and wandered through art museums. I was drawn to the vibrant colors of the Impressionists. A painting by Van Gogh or scenes by Cézanne transported me to imaginary worlds.

I fell in love with the theatre, especially plays that shed light on the human condition. When I began to connect with people from this more authentic place, I learned I could be a leader—not by exerting my will, but by nurturing the spirit I was able to see in others. And that was the inspiration that led me to a career in directing.

At rehearsal, I could feel the rise and fall of every emotion. Without fail, an actor would come over to me and whisper, "I can see the entire play, moment by moment, on your face." It became a bit of a joke, but I couldn't help it. I was so tuned into the action on stage that the rest of the world just disappeared.

I continue to be an extrovert, even a little dramatic, but I've gained confidence in the rich inner life that I used to keep hidden. It is the thread that helped me blossom as a woman and has run throughout my life.

Last week, I saw a Sondheim performance, and the songs moved me to tears. "Why am I being so sensitive?" I thought. And then I remembered: This is who I am. Sorry Sarah Heartburn, my parents loved you, but I am something more. I'm a Highly Sensitive Person. HSP for short.

First Day of School

When we moved to Long Island in November of 1952, I was five years old, and the school year had already begun. On my first day at North Side, I got all dressed up in a starched cotton dress with a green and white pinafore bib. "I'm ready, mommy," I proudly declared. My mother sat me down at the kitchen table. "Finish your cream of rice before it gets cold," she instructed, "and then we'll go."

My mother was a pretty, no-nonsense kind of woman, and I knew better than to argue with her. I finished my cereal and looked up at her for approval. "O.K.," she granted, "Wash your hands and we'll go." There was no driving this first grader to school. I was going to learn to walk, and she would show me the way.

Sydell Horowitz, 1953

We left the house, and my mother took my hand. I felt so special having her all to myself, without my older sister hogging the attention. "First, you'll go up this long, steep hill." We did it together, and it was an easy climb. When we got to the top, my mother and I turned right, and then she stopped.

"Do you see that red brick building up ahead?" she asked. I nodded my head dutifully. It had four white columns guarding the wide steps that led to the front door. "Just go through the door and ask for the principal's office," she instructed. "He'll take you right to your classroom." She leaned down and kissed me on the cheek. I could smell her signature perfume. I reached up to hug her back. As usual, she pulled away first.

I was scared. I didn't know anyone and hoped they wouldn't make fun of my curly red hair and deeply freckled face. "Bye, Mommy," I called out, but she was already out of view. "Have a good day," I heard her call back in the distance.

I gathered my courage and walked the rest of the way alone. I heard laughter on the playground in front of the school. I ran up the steps and found the office with no trouble. The principal took me to my classroom, and I settled in. "Whew, I did it," I thought. That was the first time I realized I would always be able to make it on my own.

4

Camp Cejwin

The Catskill Mountains were a hotspot for sleepaway camps in the 1950s and 60s. Just two hours from Manhattan, its sloping hillsides and flowering trees bloom all summer long. Hidden between the branches, in the sleepy town of Port Jervis, is the beautiful Lake Martin.

One side of the lake is roped off into swimming areas, and the other holds canoes tied to the dock. A wooden stairway is built into a hill about 200 feet away. When you reach the top, there's a swarm of white cabins with pull-up shades painted green.

Inside Bunk 18 sits a long-legged, freckle-faced girl with a ponytail grabbing her thick, curly hair. That's me, and I'm sitting on the floor, playing Jacks with two of my friends. I toss the small, red ball in the air and pick up two at a time, until it's Jackie's turn, and then Trudy's.

A loudspeaker announces that it's time for lunch. We all get up to go to the Mess Hall. But we don't walk — oh no — we link arms and do the "Wizard of Oz" skip, singing and laughing the whole way there.

Sydell Horowitz 1961

We find our table, and after "Hamotzi," it's time for some group spirit. The long-legged girl is, of course, the song leader. I stand on a bench and lead about 60 girls in song. Soon, another girl gets up and leads her group in a song. And so it goes until all 200 girls get to participate.

The best day of the week is Shabbat. On Friday night, we wear white tops and blue shorts. The blue is for Israel since the camp was founded by Zionists. This Friday night, I'm the Sabbath Queen. I stand at the microphone and sing my favorite prayer: "The sun on the tree-tops no longer is seen. Come gather to welcome the Sabbath, our Queen…" And after a few more verses, everyone joins in with the Hebrew.

On Shabbat day, we wear all white. After breakfast, we walk by the lake to the boys' side for services. The synagogue/auditorium holds about 600, with boys sitting on one side and girls on the other. I love singing all the familiar prayers and feeling part of the camp community. Sometimes, after services, we have Israeli dancing to get our "shpilkes" out.

And lunch? Yes, the waitresses bring lunch once we're back on the girls' side. But who cares about food at sleepaway camp? We have counselors instead of parents, and we're singing or dancing or playing all day long.

For eight weeks each summer, I went to camp in the Catskills. At home, I was always too much—too loud, too sassy, too smart for my own good. But for 13 summers, I could be myself. And that, I learned, was more than enough. Ahhh Camp Cejwin, I miss you so much!

Cheerleading

I'd like to say that being a cheerleader made me popular in high school. But I went to Wheatley, where being smart and perceptive was held in higher esteem. It was the 1960s, and our troops were in Vietnam. Folk singers like Joan Baez and Bob Dylan were calling for social justice. So, even though I was cute in my perky red and white outfit, nobody really paid attention.

Nonetheless, I had a loud voice and more energy than I knew what to do with, so being a cheerleader worked for me. I loved basketball, and whenever a player scored, one of us would jump up in front of the bleachers to do a routine. "Yay Johnny, yay Kotcher, yay, yay Johnny Kotcher!" The crowd cheered, followed by big applause. And I have to admit, I loved applause.

I was the only cheerleader who could do a cartwheel and go directly into a split. When a player scored, that was my routine. I knew the feel of the floor in our gym and how to seamlessly slide into the split.

At our first away game, I was in for a surprise. Our team scored the first basket, and I got up to do my fancy routine. The cartwheel was perfect, but when I tried to slide into the split, my heel got caught in the rubber mat in front of the stands. When I finally freed it, instead of going gracefully into the split, I slammed down with all my might. And I couldn't get up!

Talk about players getting injured in a game: I was the first Wheatley cheerleader who had to be carried off the court. Granted, it was among cheers and applause, but it was embarrassing, nonetheless.

But here's the silver lining: instead of being put on a stretcher, I was carried off by the senior class president, who was tall and handsome and my ticket to popularity.

Sydell Horowitz, 1962

I went to the hospital, where I stayed for a week because I'd pulled some muscles and broken my ischium bone. I had visitors and cards every day, and since it was less than a year since my mother had died, I relished the attention.

What could have been humiliating became a blessing. I was a sophomore, and when I went back to school on crutches, everyone knew my name and wanted to be my friend.

The President's Been Shot

The passing bell rang at 1:35 on Friday afternoon. The halls at Wheatley High were packed with teenagers opening their lockers and slamming them shut. Pretty girls with practiced smiles called out, "Hi Jan" or "Sue" or "Barb" from across the corridor. It was an assembly day, so we were returning to homeroom to check in before going to the auditorium.

As I inched my way through the crowded hall, I heard a boy from my Honors English class shout, "The president's been shot!"

"The president of the school?" I called back.

But he was gone. Then, I heard it again.

"Kennedy's been shot! The president's been SHOT!"

By the time I got to homeroom, Mr. Witt was trying to calm everyone down.

"We have no details yet," he told us. "But the president's been shot in Dallas. Let's move quietly to the assembly, and I'm sure we'll find out more."

President John F. Kennedy & Jackie Kennedy

Mr. Loring, affectionately called "Boring Loring" by his students, was at the podium. He quieted us down and addressed all 800 students at once.

"We just got word that President Kennedy has been shot on a motorcade in Texas," he said. "He's been taken to the hospital in critical condition."

We all looked at each other in shock and disbelief as we started asking questions. "Is he dead?" "Who shot him?" "Was Jackie with him?" "What hospital?"

Mr. Loring shushed us and spoke with solemnity.

"The school busses are outside waiting. You will be dismissed now and taken home. May God be with you."

We scrambled to the busses, and I made my way home. The house was empty. My mother had died two years earlier, my sister was already married, and my father was at work in Manhattan.

It was 2 p.m. I turned on the TV in the den of our cookie-cutter home on Long Island. The headlines splashed across the small screen: "John F. Kennedy has been shot dead." "The 35th president of the United States has been assassinated." Walter Cronkite, the stalwart of network broadcasting, was crying as he quietly reported the news.

My heart skips a beat. I'm no stranger to bad news, but I'm alone in the house and have no way to process it. The TV flashes with images of Jackie leaning over her husband in an open convertible. Her hands and face are covered in blood as she tries to hold onto him. Cut to Parkland Hospital in Dallas, showing Jackie in tears with her husband's blood all over her dress. Then back again to the motorcade with the president sitting on top of the back seat smiling broadly as he waved to his adoring fans. Who could predict that in two minutes' time, he would suffer the most brutal of fates? The images keep playing on a continuous loop.

I've always known that life was fragile, but at 16, I was reminded again. Kennedy was the hope of a new generation. We rallied around him and held tight to his words of inspiration.

The TV screen flashes again as it cuts to Lyndon B. Johnson, that tired old senator who became VP so he could rally the Southern vote for JFK. Jackie is in the picture, and her husband's blood has still not been washed off. She stands opposite LBJ as he's sworn in as the 36th president of the United States.

I'm in shock. How quickly a new leader has been put in place. Will the memory of JFK be abandoned the same way my mother's was?

I rock back and forth on the green tweed couch in the den. I've forgotten how to cry, so I just stare in disbelief.

"The king is dead. Long live the king."

My Mother's Story

We are all shaped by our history, and Janet's was steeped in love. But it was also laced with trauma, the kind that passes from one generation to the next. Janet's parents were forced to leave their homes when the Russian Empire expelled the Jews in 1911. Her father, Abraham Kay (Kossofsky) emigrated from Kiev, and her mother, Edith Garelick, from Belarus.

Janet Kay Horowitz, 1947

They landed in New York and were married on December 22, 1913, when Edith was 17 and Abe was 21. As immigrants, they had to learn a new language and scramble to find a means of support. Edith's sisters were married off and scattered to different parts of the country. But Abe had a cousin in Rochester, so that's where they settled.

Their first child was born on May 5, 1917, and they named her Janet. Three years later, her sister Alice was born, and Beverly six years after that. Rochester is a beautiful city in upstate New York, where Janet learned to appreciate opera and horseback riding. She was a good student, but by the time she was ten, the family moved 300 miles away. Abe wanted to open his own factory in the garment district, and that meant moving to Brooklyn.

Janet adored her father and made friends easily, so the move went smoothly for her. She was pretty, poised, and popular, and by the time she was in high school, she attracted the attention of many young men. She was also a born leader and took great satisfaction in running a girls' club for young teens who needed a big sister.

In 1937, she met Milton Horowitz. He may not have been as handsome as some of her boyfriends, but he had a great sense of humor and was smart as a whip. She was the refined, beautiful girl from Rochester, falling in love with the boy from the Lower East Side. But Milton had just finished law school, showered her with attention, and kept her laughing. And judging from the smiles in pictures of their early days together, he made her feel like the most beautiful girl in the world. It was clear they were a match and were married on March 24, 1940, in New York City, when Janet was 22 and Milt was 25.

The wedding was an exquisite, formal affair with nine bridesmaids in matching silk gowns and nine groomsmen in tuxedos. Janet and Milton were the oldest in their respective families, and her parents loved him immediately. Wages were low in 1940, but Milt got a raise to $6.00 a week as a law clerk when they got married, and Janet worked as a bookkeeper. They honeymooned in Florida and returned to an apartment in the Bensonhurst neighborhood of Brooklyn.

They lived on the same block as Janet's sister Alice and husband Jess, as well as her parents, and they all became close. This made for a happy first year as "Janet Horowitz," and on May 6, 1943, it got even better. One day after her 26th birthday, Nancy Roberta was born, and the couple became a family. The war in Europe was escalating, but Milt thought he'd be exempt from serving since he was a lawyer and had a new baby. Nonetheless, when Nancy was six months old, Milt was drafted into the Army.

Janet followed her husband to North Carolina while he was in basic training. But when he was shipped overseas in 1944, she returned to New York and worked for WAVES (Women Accepted for Volunteer Emergency Services). It was difficult raising her daughter alone, but when Milton returned in 1946, they went on a second honeymoon to Miami Beach to celebrate.

Their second daughter, Sydell, was born on February 18, 1947, when Janet was 29. Alice and Jess had two sons almost the same age as Janet's daughters, so everyone shared responsibilities. It was a happy time for her, being close to family and staying home with her girls. Milt was doing well in his law practice in Manhattan, so in 1951, they snuck away on a vacation to Toronto and Lake George, where Janet got to do some horseback riding. But it was when Milt bought her a mink coat that she knew she had arrived. In the 1950's, it was a huge status symbol, and she was proud to be the wife of a successful lawyer.

Janet was ambitious, not only for herself but for her daughters. Nancy was especially pretty, and Janet took her into Manhattan to get professional pictures so she could do some modeling. Nancy did well, and when Sydell turned five, Janet got pictures for her too. But by 1952, the family was moving to the suburbs of Long Island, and going 30 miles into the city for photo shoots was just too much.

The new house in Mineola was Janet's dream, and when they moved in, she was delighted. They didn't see their families as often, but they got together for the Jewish holidays. There were always at least 20 around the table, the food was plentiful, and the atmosphere was warm. Once Janet settled into suburban life, she and Milt got involved in building a new synagogue. She became president of the Sisterhood and began volunteering at many charitable organizations. She was a volunteer at Long Island Jewish Hospital and became president of the local chapter of The United Cerebral Palsy Association. She was great at organizing meetings and events and loved entertaining friends at her home.

Her father's business was growing, but he needed money to expand and open a new factory. He could get a loan from a cousin, but only if Milton cosigned. To please Janet, Milt did so, without giving it a second thought. But on a December morning in 1954, Janet got a phone call that rocked her world. Her father, Abraham Kay, had been found dead in his factory. They assumed it was a heart attack, but when they found him the next morning, he was hanging from a rope, having taken his own life.

Apparently, Abe's loan had come due, and he didn't have the money to pay it back. It's hard to know all the details, because it was kept secret for many years. Did he want to spare Janet and Milt from the financial burden? Was Abe embezzling money from the factory? Was Edith somehow complicit? Nonetheless, seeing no other way out, on December 4, 1954, Abraham Kay ended his life. This was traumatic for Janet, who adored her father, but she fought to maintain a façade and kept the shameful secret to herself.

There is a lot written about the relationship between mind and body when it comes to disease. Could the trauma of her father's suicide have activated a dormant genetic anomaly? Regardless of the root cause, fourteen months later, when Janet was 38, she was diagnosed with breast cancer. She was a no-nonsense woman and matter-of-factly told her daughters that she was going to the hospital to have a breast removed. Nancy was twelve, and Sydell was nine, but the word "cancer" was never used, and she reassured them that everything would be fine.

Fortunately, Janet recovered well from the surgery, and life continued as if nothing had gone wrong. The family went on vacation to Washington, D.C., where everyone had fun, and no mention was made of her recent mastectomy.

In 1956, you couldn't put an ad for a breast cancer support group in the New York Times because it contained two words that were censored: breast and cancer. So, to help other women who'd had the same surgery, Janet made a point of visiting them in the hospital. She comforted them and willingly gave her friendship. Ruth Schwartz was one such woman. Their families became close, and Ruth became a trusted friend for many years to come.

By 1957, Janet's hospital work came to a sudden halt. There was a lump in her other breast. The doctor told Milt that it was probably Janet's breast cancer coming back, but removing her other breast would be too upsetting for her. There was no chemotherapy in those days, so without including Janet or her daughters, the doctor and Milt chose to treat it with radiation. In those days, husbands made decisions for their wives. They often decided if the wife should even be told the truth about her diagnosis. Janet was not told. And her sister's husbands decided not to tell their wives either.

By the end of 1958, the atmosphere around the home changed as the cancer silently progressed. Janet's health and state of mind were both unpredictable. She was in and out of the hospital with "calcium deposits," but somehow, she always recovered. There were days when she was quite ill and others when she got dressed in her nylons and heels to attend a charity luncheon or a game of mahjong. On her bad days, she was short-tempered and frequently irritated by her daughters, who were also kept from the truth. She yelled at them and seemed to blow up over the smallest infractions. On her good days, however, she would play her opera records and bustle around the house singing along. She continued to get her long, beautiful nails manicured in her signature bright red, and she also remained ambitious for her girls.

In 1959, Janet took 12-year-old Sydell into Manhattan to enroll her in the American Academy of Dramatic Arts. Nancy had been the model, but Sydell would be the actress. Going alone on the train into the city was fun for Sydell and kept her distracted from what was going on at home. Janet was weakening, but she still had her good days. She was proud of her daughters and enjoyed planning Sydell's Bat Mitzvah in February of 1960. At 42, she remained a gracious hostess and looked beautiful at the party, although in some of the pictures, one of her eyes seemed to be closing.

The cancer had reached her brain by that time, and nobody said a word. Several months later, when Janet became so sick that she had to be rushed to the hospital, the cover-up continued. It was hepatitis, she was told this time, and everyone went along. By February of 1961, Janet had more bad days than good. Nonetheless, she and Milt celebrated the five-year anniversary of her mastectomy as evidence that she was cancer-free.

But by May, she had taken a turn for the worse. One day, she called Sydell to help her get out of bed to go to the bathroom; Janet was so weak, she fell right there on the floor. A neighbor came to help her up, and a nurse was hired to assist her during the day. But no conversation took place in the family. Milt went to work, and the girls went to school, and it was never acknowledged that she was dying of cancer.

Inevitably, on May 26, 1961, just weeks after turning 44, Janet Kay Horowitz passed away. She left two daughters, then 14 and 18, with no explanation or words of goodbye. Did she know she was dying? Did she know that the cancer had returned? Or was the need to be strong more important than the truth? Cancer was whispered about in those days, and breast cancer, in particular, was stigmatized as a curse. There were no marathons, pink ribbons, or celebrities trumpeting their cause. There were only secrets and lies. And in that environment, the life of my mother was cut short.

Family with Sydell in the carriage, 1948

Just as illness was kept secret in the 1950's, so was grief. After Janet died, her husband couldn't talk about her, so her children followed suit. They didn't want to upset him for fear of losing their one remaining parent. Milton held on to old resentments and cut off his relationship with her mother and eventually her sisters. They still lived in Brooklyn and remained distant for many years to come. The memories began to fade, and her name was rarely mentioned. But her life mattered, and she deserves to be remembered.

Janet Kay Horowitz was a beauty in her youth, a leader in her community, ambitious for her children, and a proud and loving wife. She was tall and slim with shiny black hair. She wore Donna Reed shirt-waist dresses with high heels and was always confident in social situations. She loved her parents and her sisters and their children and was equally warm to her husband's extended family. She was strong and efficient and always tried to look her best and do what was expected. When she was well, she cooked dinner in dresses and heels and never complained.

My mother would be proud of the legacy she left behind. Her husband of 22 years found love again and continued to make people laugh. Nancy married Ruth Schwartz's son and had three beautiful children, who all distinguished themselves in their careers. Nancy had four grandchildren, whom Janet would have loved.

I went to Yale Drama School and became a theatre professor, thanks to my mother's push, and then a marriage and family therapist. My son is a rabbi, a hospital chaplain, and a leader in his community. My daughter has the poise and confidence of her grandmother, with a successful career to boot. Between the two of them, I have seven beautiful grandchildren.

Janet Horowitz's life may have been all too short, but as her youngest daughter, I refuse to let her memory be forgotten.

AUTHOR REFLECTION

It's been over 60 years since my mother died. When I began to write "My Mother's Story" in 2016, family and friends from her generation were long gone. She was rarely mentioned by my father or even my sister, and the memories had begun to fade.

I had boxes of pictures that relatives had given me over the years. I pulled out all the photos and tried to arrange them chronologically. I knew my mother was born in Rochester, so I studied the backgrounds in her childhood pictures. I was able to guess what activities she liked and when her family moved to Brooklyn.

I found her wedding pictures, which gave me even more details. My father, who died in 2002 at 88 years old, had never spoken of it. Once he remarried, five years after she passed, the subject of my mother became taboo. In fact, my father's dying words to me were how Lila, his second wife, was the love of his life.

When I wrote my mother's story, I sent my sister the first draft. She confirmed some of the details for accuracy, but our feelings surrounding that time in our lives had never been broached. Nancy lives in Florida, and I live in California, so our visits over the years had been sporadic. But three years ago, when she had a minor surgery, I stayed with her for a week to help her convalesce. It gave me the opportunity to bring up some long-hidden memories that I needed to share.

One morning, Nancy asked me to help her wash her hair in the sink. As I scrubbed her scalp, I had an image of my mother watching her two girls taking care of each other. "Mommy would be so happy to see us together right now," I whispered, speaking the only name we had ever used for her. Nancy warmed and began to smile, so I went on. "I always think of the morning she died. She was sleeping, and I tip-toed out of the house so I wouldn't wake her and have to get her pills. I wish I had stopped and at least said goodbye."

My sister sighed, "I must have left after you. I went into her room and asked her how she felt. 'A little better,' she answered, which is what she always said to me. And then I told her, 'Good. I love you.'"

It was like the sun had finally come out from behind the shadows. "Oh, Nancy," I said, "I'm so happy she got that from one of her daughters. That must have been the last thing she heard before she died."

Rewriting my mother's story for this "Gone Too Soon" anthology made me realize that most of what I remember about her life revolved around her death. I didn't get to tell her then, but I hope that sharing her story is a way to say "I love you" now.

Somehow, I think she already knew.

Family Secrets

I grew up on Long Island in a house that held a world of secrets. And my father was the secret keeper.

When I was nine years old, my mother went to the hospital to have surgery. I remember her telling me that she was having a breast removed. I didn't have breasts yet, so the concept was foreign to me. And since my father said it wasn't serious, I never really worried. But when I turned 11, I started having nightmares. One night, I woke up screaming because I was sure my mother was dead.

Janet Kay Horowitz, 1959

I ran downstairs crying and climbed into my parents' bed. It was cozy cuddled between them, and they reassured me that everything was fine. It was my father who said, "Dreams like that are a sign that Mommy will live a long life." And I believed them. Even though my mother kept going in and out of the hospital, she always seemed to get better.

But lately, she'd become short-tempered and yelled at me a lot. If I dropped something on the floor or, made the dog bark, or ran up to my room where she couldn't catch me, I would get in trouble. I knew it was my fault. I'd become a bratty 12-year-old, and as hard as I tried, I just couldn't behave any better.

When I was 13, my mother was hospitalized for longer. This time, I was told it was hepatitis, and again, my father said it wasn't serious. But when she came home, she could barely get out of bed. The beautiful, stylish woman she once was had disappeared. In her place was a frail, graying woman I barely recognized. She was 43, which seemed old to me, so I figured that's what happens when you age.

One afternoon, right after I turned 14, my mother called to me from her bedroom downstairs. I ran down as fast as I could. As I entered her room, a small voice spoke to me in the dark. "Come here, Sydell. I need your help." I felt the air thicken like dark clouds on a gloomy day.

My mother tried to sit up, but all I could see was a cloud of maroon. As I got closer to the bed, the maroon morphed into my mother's bathrobe, the one with the white piping. "I need help getting to the bathroom," said the weak, whispering voice. As I sat on the edge of the bed, I could see up close how thin and pale she was. Why hadn't I paid more attention? My mother was not an affectionate woman. I barely remembered being hugged as a child. What I did remember is her familiar refrain whenever a child was crying: "Don't pick her up. You'll spoil her."

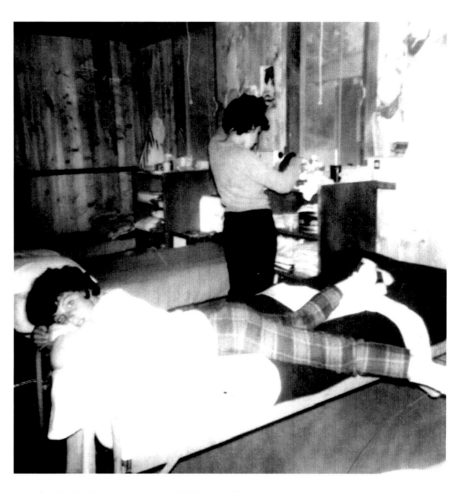

Sydell Horowitz, 1961 (at Camp, six weeks after my mother died)

Her voice interrupted my thoughts. "I'm going to put my left arm around your neck if you can hold me under my right." As I leaned over, pink and green and purple clouded my vision. I blinked and saw it was her lamp, the one with the urn base and antique globe shade.

I put my hand under my mother's arm. The skin felt shriveled, like a balloon that had just deflated. I stood slowly, trying to bear her weight. Even though I was skinny, I managed to get a good grip. I tried standing up slowly, but as soon as I took a step, my mother fell to the floor in a heap of maroon.

"Oh no. How could I have dropped her?" I thought. My mother looked up and spoke to me in a firm voice. "Get Mr. Hyman next door," she instructed. I ran out of the house, with my mother on the floor, and started banging on my neighbor's door.

Mr. Hyman was a big man with kind eyes, and he came immediately. He easily lifted my mother back onto her bed. He made a phone call, and before long, the bedroom was filled with paramedics. Without noticing me, the paramedics put her on a stretcher and wheeled her out of the house.

My father met them at the hospital and brought my mother home the next day. He told my sister and me that he'd hired a nurse to look after her in the afternoon. He convinced us that she'd be fine just as soon as she regained her strength.

Two weeks later, on May 26, 1961, the phone buzzed in my English class. Mr. Witt answered it and looked very serious. When he hung up, he said calmly, "Sydell, dear, please take all your books with you and go to the principal's office." I was embarrassed by my classmates' attention, but I headed out the door. Before I got to the office, I saw my big sister in the opposite direction. "Come on, Syd," she said. "Daddy's waiting for us outside."

My father was out front, and my sister got into the passenger seat of the car as I slipped into the back. As he started to drive, he finally told me the truth. "Mommy's had breast cancer for the past five years," he said. "She's at the hospital in a coma, but she'll probably be gone by the time we get there."

I began to cry, big heaving sobs that I thought would never end. Alone in the back seat, there were no arms to hold me close, no hands to stroke my hair, no words to give me comfort. My mind began to spin. "I was such a brat. How could I have not known? I should have been nicer to her. Was it my fault for aggravating her?" And from that moment on, I knew these feelings of guilt would haunt me for the rest of my life.

A few minutes later, we arrived at the hospital, and I followed my father to the elevator. When we got out on the third floor, I saw my grandparents and my mother's two sisters sitting in the waiting room with their heads down, unable to make eye contact.

My father walked to the nurse's station while I waited behind. Tears rolled down his face when they told him my mother was gone. But he refused the offer to visit her room, an offer that was not extended to me or my sister.

I leaned on the wall some ten feet away. I never said goodbye, or apologized for being fresh, or told her I loved her. And the pain was more than my 14-year-old psyche could bear. So slowly, imperceptibly, I felt myself leave my body and watch the scene from above.

It was quiet in the house on the morning after my mother died. I followed my father down to the basement, where he was doing laundry. It was odd to see him doing housework. That was my mother's job, not his. "Daddy," I implored, "I don't understand. You always told me she'd get better."

He was facing the washing machine with his back to me. "She's in heaven now, Delky. That's all you need to know." I loved when he called me Delky, from the Dell part of Sydell. But it wasn't enough to make me feel better. "Where's heaven?" I asked with mounting desperation. "Will I get to see her or talk to her again?"

There was a long silence while I waited for an explanation; I was lost and confused. Finally, my father turned around. "She was sick for a really long time. It's over now. Just be glad she's out of pain." He turned back to the washing machine and measured out the detergent. "Go upstairs. I'll be there soon."

But my mind was spinning. "Why didn't I know she was dying? Was it my fault? I know I was bad. What if Daddy dies? Where will I live?" But the feelings were too much, so I went to the fridge and looked for something sweet. Nothing. Only apples, oranges, and some rancid-looking cottage cheese.

And then I remembered the cookies in the drawer next to the sink. Bingo! An unopened box of Oreos stared me in the face. I tore off the wrapper, split the cookie apart, and licked out the creamy filling. Ahhh. I immediately felt better. I take another and another, ravenously licking out the filling and then eating the round cookies piled on the side.

Suddenly I heard a noise; it was my father coming up from the basement. I grabbed the box and hurried upstairs to my room. I wolfed down the rest of the cookies like the answer to life was hiding at the bottom. When I was done, I felt calmer, much calmer, and less overwhelmed.

And just like that, less than 24 hours after my mother died, I learned how to manage my feelings. My father wasn't the only one who kept secrets.

Dadky

My father called me Delky from the "dell" part of Sydell, and I called him Dadky. He was a funny, playful man, and we had our own private banter. He'd begin with, "I wuv ooo Delk..." "-ky" I'd answer. "I wuv ooo Dad..." "-ky" he'd reply. This was always followed by laughter or tickling or a shout out to the dog, who got excited by our little show.

As a child, I was the light of his life. My father used to come upstairs and tuck me in at night. He didn't read books to me, like other parents did with their kids. He would tell me stories instead, and he always made ME the heroine. His bright, attentive eyes seemed to mirror my expressions and made me feel like nothing mattered more than what I had to say.

We also looked alike, with the same Horowitz red hair and freckles. My hair color was toned down thanks to my mother's good genes. My father and I were both outgoing and loved to sing and perform and be the center of attention. Yes, I was definitely Milty's daughter, and I wore that title proudly.

His friends loved him for his "Milton Berle" personality. As the son of immigrants, he worked his way through law school doing comedy in the Borscht Belt. Even though my mother seemed to favor my sister, my father and I were thick as thieves.

Sydell and Milton, 1970

When my mother died, I was 14 years old. On the night of her passing, my father came upstairs and slept in the other twin bed in my room. It's something I'll never forget. When my sister got married a year later, my father and I became even closer. On Saturdays, I'd ride shotgun with him on his errands, telling him every detail of my life along the way.

When I had cheerleading practice in the basement of our house, he'd come downstairs and show us his cheers from Boys High in Brooklyn. "Boom chicka boom, boom chicka boom, Booooys High!" My friends didn't say, "Poor Sydell, growing up without a mother." Instead, there was, "Let's go to Sydell's. Her dad is so much fun."

For five years, I had my father all to myself. But when I went away to college, he finally started dating. And why not? He was only 47 when my mother died, and besides being good-looking, he was a successful Park Avenue attorney. Nonetheless, when he called to tell me he was getting married, I was taken by surprise. I hadn't even met the woman, and the wedding was going to be in six weeks.

From that point on, everything happened fast. I met Lila twice, my childhood home was sold, and after a tasteful Sunday wedding at the Roslyn Country Club, we moved into her house. Lila had two children who naturally came with the deal. Her son was my age, 19, and her daughter Karen was an awkward 14.

My father's been gone since 2002; I miss him terribly. He loved and nurtured me the first 19 years of my life, and that can never be erased. I have beautiful children and grandchildren, I'm widowed, and I live alone.

When I'm struggling with a difficult task, I hear a voice in my head saying, "Come on Delky, you can do it." It's the strength I learned from my father. And it always reminds me that he's the reason I knew that I was worthy of love.

Sydell and Milton, 1992

Lila's Home

I sit down at the round glass table on my stepmother's back porch. It's enclosed on all sides by jalousie windows, the kind with horizontal slats that open out like vents. Lila, my father's new wife, calls it the Jalousie Room. I remember the finished back porch at my childhood home, but my mother never gave the rooms names.

I'm having dinner with Lila, her daughter Karen, and my father. My father and I, or Dadky as I called him, were especially close since my mother died five years ago. But I'm 19 now, my childhood home has been sold, and I'm expected to be part of his new family.

Milton and Lila

Lila calls out to the kitchen, "Blanche, dear. Please clear the salad plates and bring out the roast." Blanche is the middle-aged black servant who lives with them. She is a tall woman with short dark hair who only speaks when spoken to. It's 1966, and the civil rights movement is raging across the country. And this is what's going on in my home. I try to contain my feelings to avoid upsetting my father's life.

The conversation remains superficial, peppered with my father teasing 14-year-old Karen. "Hey, Ka, look at your left ear," he chirps. "Oops, here's a quarter I just found in there!" Karen laughs and grabs the quarter. "Wait, do that again, Pop," she says. "Pop?" I think. No way am I going to call Lila anything but her name. "Dadky," I interject, "want to hear about the classes I'm taking this fall?" "Tell me later, Delk," he says dismissively as he makes another quarter appear out of Karen's right ear.

My father and Karen continue laughing at this new trick as I quietly finish my dinner. "One more week," I calculate, "and then I can go back to college." I look over at Lila, who is thrilled to see her daughter bonding with my dad, and I ask, "Can I please be excused from the table?" It's a formality that wasn't required in my home. I'm granted permission and go up to my room to escape.

The room I've been given is no more than 10x10 and painted a neutral beige. All my personal things – as well as my mother's – were packed away in boxes in the basement, unlikely to resurface any time soon. I sit on the bed, which has bolsters along the back to look like a couch, making it easier to convert the room back into an office when I return to school.

It feels so different from the bedroom I grew up in. My room was a converted attic with yellow wallpaper that my mother let me pick out. The drawers were built into the angled walls, and my desk was in front of the dormered window.

I take off my shoes and the face I had to wear during dinner and let the tears come. There is not one picture or piece of furniture or dishes or knick-knacks from my home. It's like my past has been erased and my mother's life obliterated.

I sit there alone in the small beige room. I don't belong here. I feel like I'm collateral damage in my father's new family. Nobody's really interested in how I feel. My heart is broken, and I feel alone and ignored. But my father's attention is focused on Karen, and there it remains for the next 36 years.

I've learned how to survive on my own. If nothing else, losing my mother taught me resilience. So I go back to school, finish my degree, and head to Yale Drama School. When I get married at 23, my husband and I move to California and create a life of our own. I have children, find a community, and have a successful career.

But the truth remains. I lost my mother at 14. And when I was 19, I lost my father.

Chapter Two

Finding My Way

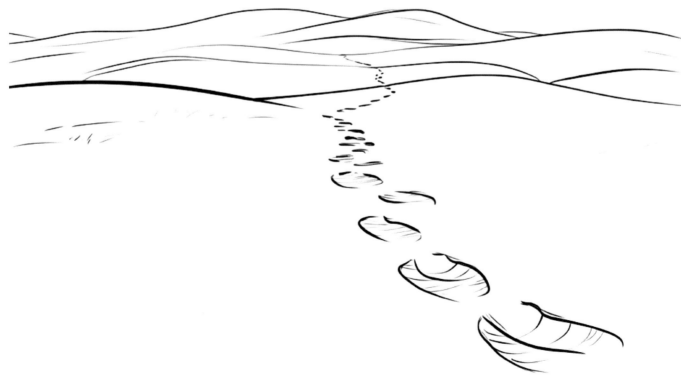

I am Who I am

My sister Nancy loved tomato soup, and so did my mom. It wasn't my favorite. But I ate it anyway to avoid being scolded and told, "You don't know what good is!" And it wasn't just about food. My mother and sister seemed to have a secret society to which I didn't belong. I was the baby born after the war, and my sister was born before.

When my father was drafted in 1943, my mother was left alone with my sister for almost two years. Maybe that was the bond I didn't understand. Nancy was pretty as a child and even looked like my mom – with her pale skin, wavy hair, and flawless complexion.

I was smart and funny like my dad. I had his curly reddish hair and a face full of freckles, too numerous to count. My father called me "monkey face," which was supposed to be cute. But I thought I looked like a female version of Howdy Doody.

When I look back at pictures of myself during my first six years, I was adorable. But my sister was the one who got all the oohs and ahhs, and I was the freckled face kid with personality. In the 1950's and 60's, the most important attribute for a girl was her looks, so she could find herself a good husband.

Sydell Horowitz, as Rebecca West in 1965

But I wanted more. And fortunately, my world changed when I turned seventeen.

I went away to college and discovered that I was not only smart but also talented and pretty. And the shock stunned and amazed me! I had always been in plays, but once I got to college, I became the darling of the theatre department.

I got the lead in every main-stage production, and I began to thrive. I was the Bride in Lorca's *Blood Wedding*, Juno in O'Casey's *Juno and the Paycock*, Jenny Diver in *Three Penny Opera*, and Rebecca West in *Ibsen's Rosmersholm*.

My years at Binghamton University, or State University of New York at Binghamton, were some of the happiest of my life. As I came into my own, it became clear that theatre would be

This Woman Runs the Show!

By Pamela McCovey
Staff Writer

The Women's Dialogue Association of CSU Dominguez Hills will be presenting a series of dialogues about the issues affecting contemporary women.

On October 17, Sydell Weiner, a threatre arts lecturer at CSUDH, will speak on "Women's Perspective in Theatre Arts." The dialogue will take place in the President's Conference Room in the E.R.C. building. "I will be

Sydell Weiner

focusing on women in theatre and what the situation is like in Hollywood today," said Weiner.

Although Weiner will be discussing women's perspective in theatre, Weiner's main interest is in the art of directing. "I've always been interested in the theatre," she said. "I really became interested in directing in junior high school."

A native born New Yorker, Weiner studied in New York at The American Academy of Drama Arts. She then went on to Yale Drama School in New Haven, Connecticut.

Weiner explained that she did a lot of acting in New York, but decided to come to California where she has acted in some commercials as well as directing several.

Weiner has been a director for ten years, but this is only her second year at CSUDH, where she finds the students in the Arts Department to be "willing, anxious and ready to work."

"I like the atmosphere at CSUDH," she added. "There is a multi-racial mixture of students who are very energetic."

A woman in her thirties, Weiner has found the role of directing exciting and a challenge. "I find it easier to see how things work. It's harder for women to direct since directing is traditionally a man's job.

"In being an actor, there is no way to tell how the performance is going," she explained. "I enjoy being able to see the performance out of other actors, rather than acting and trying to see how my performance is being conducted.

"I love being able to shape the performance," she added. "The whole and overview of a performance makes a statement."

We will get a chance to see her work in November 8th-9th, and 15th-17th when "You Can't Take It With You," will be performed in the Theatre Department at CSUDH. Weiner explained that the play is a "comedy play, a classic comedy, based on two families with opposing lifestyles." Weiner promises the play will be enjoyable to everyone. The dialogues will start at 11:45 a.m. and end at 1:30 p.m. and will take place in the University Center.

Sydell, Cal State Dominguez Hills, 1985

at the center of my life. I went to Yale Drama School and earned a PhD from N.Y.U., and soon figured out how to have a career that I loved and still make a good living.

I was smart enough to be a lawyer like my dad, but that wasn't really an option for girls at the time. So, I followed my heart and found a creative path instead. I'm sure it was one my father would have loved. But as the oldest son of poor Jewish immigrants, he was destined to go in a different direction.

I still don't like tomato soup, but it no longer matters. My sister took after my mom, and I took after my dad. Having been so young when my mother died, I looked to my father as a role model. I like to think that I was living out his dream or what might have been his true calling. Because, without a doubt, it was his inspiration that helped me find my own way.

The Summer of 1969

It was the summer of 1969. We sang peace and love at Woodstock. A man walked on the moon. And our boys were fighting a senseless war in Vietnam.

I was getting over a rough breakup with a complicated, James Dean kind of guy. So, when I heard they needed a Drama Counselor at my old summer camp, I jumped at the chance to get away. The Catskill Mountains had always been my refuge, so off I went.

The first week of camp, I met a nice, uncomplicated guy named Howie—a popular Jewish name in the 60s. We had the same day off and he had a car, so when he asked me to go to the County Fair, of course I said Yes.

Sydell and Howard, 1969

Howie tossed balls at plastic ducks and won me a teddy bear. We ate sticky, pink, cotton candy and went on the Ferris wheel. And then we came to the roller coaster. I had never been a fan, but it was a first date, so I agreed.

It was terrifying!

Not hands in the air, screaming for fun kind of terror. But I thought I would die. As our cart reached the highest point and then FLEW down the track, I PANICKED-- I could barely breathe. When we finally got off, I was shaking all over. Howie was gentle and took really good care of me. And before long, I fell in love with uncomplicated.

We got married the next summer because-- that's just what you did. We had two children and were happy for a while. But it turns out complicated is in my DNA. I thrived on being with people, while he liked being at home. Where I was creative, he was black and white. I tried to explain my feelings, but the answer was always the same: "I hear what you're saying, but I can't relate. My mind doesn't work that way." After 20 years, we knew it was over.

The day he moved out, we hugged each other and said, "I will always love you." And

Sydell & Howard, June 1970

thank God, it has come true. I remarried--someone complicated--and Howard (as he's called today) has a long-term girlfriend. But we have seven grandchildren and celebrate most holidays together. He's the first one I call to talk about the kids or get sound financial advice.

Howard has been a constant in my life, and I'd do anything for him. Anything, that is, except ride another roller coaster.

A Woman's Place

Her high heels clicked on the pavement as she walked across campus. The young professor was wearing a slim pencil skirt and a fitted blazer. A cream silk blouse snuck out at the collar, drawing attention to her long, slender neck. Although her outfit was from Loehmann's and not Nordstrom, she knew she looked classy.

The bold California sun filled her with hope. And when she caught her reflection in a window of the Humanities Building, the woman smiled. "How different my life is from my parents," she thought. Her parents were both children of immigrants who lived on the Lower East Side of New York. They made their way out of poverty in search of the American dream.

Sydell, 1984

She remembered coming home at 20, having just completed her B.A. Her dad tried to be helpful when he handed her The New York Times. "The best way to find a job is the want ads," he said. "Look under Gal Friday," a phrase from the 60s suggesting a faithful female assistant.

Her mother had worked as a bookkeeper before she had children. In those days, careers for women were something to "fall back on." As a stay-at-home mom, she would never have asked her husband to clear the table or wash the dishes. That was her work, and she'd have thought it demeaning for a man.

But it was 1984, and the world was changing. This Gal Monday, Tuesday, Wednesday, Thursday, and Friday was one of a handful of women PhDs on campus, a reality that would prove shocking to her own children when they were grown. Female doctors and lawyers would be commonplace. And educated women would continue to gain traction in the workforce.

Yet, to this woman, it was more than blazing a trail for the next generation. She was securing her independence. Married or not, she'd be able to take care of herself and make it on her own. Finding creative work that she loved was the icing on the cake, the part that made her heart do backflips.

Cal State Dominguez Hills Theatre Department in 1984. Sydell is the only woman

She continued across campus, feeling confident about the future. When she came to the meeting room, she stood quietly by the door.

At the head of the table sat a stylish black woman. It was Yolanda Moses who would go on to become president of City College in New York.

Yolanda smiled at me as I entered the room, and I knew that I had arrived!

Strawberries

I reach for some strawberries as my father unpacks them from his grocery bag. "No, sweetheart," he says, "those are saved for mommy." I'm 12 or 13, and my mother is sick in bed. My father reassures me that she'll get well, so I go to my room as he tends to her needs.

But she doesn't get well. She doesn't get well at all.

Three months after my fourteenth birthday, my father picks my sister and me up from school a little after noon. We have no idea until he starts driving to the hospital. On the way to the hospital, he tells us the truth he's been hiding for five years. "Mommy has breast cancer. She was rushed to the hospital this morning because she's dying. She will probably be gone by the time we get there."

When we get to the hospital, we take the elevator up to her floor. My father goes by himself to the nurse's station. It is very quiet, so I'm able to every word that is said. "I'm so sorry, your wife has passed away. Would you like to go into her room and see her?" the nurse asks matter of factly. My father replies, "No, I want to remember her alive." And then he starts to cry, big heaving sobs that sound like they'll never end.

I'm standing by myself, and all I can think of is eating a huge bowl of strawberries. I'm not physically hungry; just feel empty and shocked and abandoned. Why has my mother's cancer been kept secret from everyone but my dad? How am I supposed to deal with my feelings? What are my feelings, and who can I talk to about them?

Sydell & Janet 1956

When we leave the hospital, my father seems to close up. I don't want to upset him, so I try to act normal and go on with my life. My father hires a housekeeper to clean in the afternoons and prepare dinner. She goes about her daily tasks, rarely interacting with me. I stay up in my room and find solace in my own little secret.

When the housekeeper isn't looking, I put two pieces of thinly sliced bread together in the same slot of the toaster. When they pop up, I separate them and smooth butter on the soft, untoasted insides. "Mmm, delicious… just like freshly baked bread." I stuff down about six slices when I hear the housekeeper approaching from the hall. I tell her I'm going to the store on the corner and get out of her way.

Grabbing some money, I run down the street. When I get to the store, I stand at the counter, and my mouth starts to water. Through the glass I see the tempting treats, freshly made donuts with gooey, glazed topping. My mother didn't allow us bread with dinner, nor did we ever have sweets for dessert. We had Jello or canned fruit cocktail, or when we were lucky, fresh, whole strawberries.

I reach into my pocket and tell the clerk at the store that I want six donuts. I feel scared and guilty like I'm breaking some kind of law. I hurry home and go quickly up to my room to hide from the housekeeper. I wolf down the donuts as fast as I can, afraid if I stop that my mother will appear and grab them away from me. But she doesn't appear. She's dead. And when I finish the bag, I am relieved. I haven't been caught, and my heart finally stops racing. I've won, and for the moment, I am satisfied.

**Binge-eating is not a choice.
It's a trauma response.**

Feeling the need to be busy all the time is a trauma response and fear-based distraction from what you'd be forced to acknowledge and feel if you slowed down.

In the first year after my mother died, I gained 25 pounds. I also grew four inches, so I was able to keep it hidden. When the weight started to show, I would starve myself to compensate. I'd eat huge amounts of food and then punish myself by dieting mercilessly. Food became my best friend and worst enemy.

It's hard to believe from today's perspective, but it took me twenty years before I got any help. After years of denial, I found a therapist and started feeling my feelings. I learned healthier ways to reduce my anxiety. I began to understand my feelings of guilt and how to let go of them. And most importantly, I learned what it means to self-soothe.

Even though my eating disorder is a thing of the past, I still struggle with my relationship to food. Sometimes I'm in remission for years at a time, and then someone I love gets sick or dies, and I'm 14 years old again.

Today, I'm in a period of grace, even though I'm grieving for my husband, who died three years ago. But instead of numbing my feelings with food, I am expressing them through writing. Yes, I have learned to comfort myself by telling my truth. And to me, it's a lot more satisfying than eating donuts or forbidden bowls of strawberries.

My Father

My father was a Conservative Jew, so our house was strictly kosher. But he was also a lawyer. As a 6'2 carrot top, he knew how to win an argument. And if you didn't agree with him, he could easily prove you wrong.

I moved to California in 1970. Since my father lived in New York, I rarely shared my problems. But when my son was a teenager, he went through a rough patch. He hated school. He stayed in his room and spoke in one-word sentences.

When Jason was 20, he spent his junior year abroad in Israel. It was a life-changing experience. Yes, he found inspiration in Orthodox Judaism. But it was more than that. He became talkative again and excited about learning. It didn't matter that we were Reform. He found meaning and purpose in life, and I couldn't have been happier!

Milton and Sydell at Jason's H.S. graduation

A year later, when he decided to be a rabbi, I called my father in New York, expecting him to be proud. "Daddy," I began with excitement, "Jason's applying to rabbinical school."

"Nice," my father began, "Reform?"

"No," I answered

"Oh, Conservative!" my father said with approval.

"No… he's become Orthodox and…"

Before I could finish, my father began to rant. "Orthodox! You're kidding! They are a Cult!! Do you see them walking around? Men with their beards and women with skirts to their toes? Just wait, he'll have ten children." "So what? If that's what he wants to do?" "Oy Orthodox," my father said under his breath. "Talk to you next week, Delky."

I wanted to explain how Jason's faith took him out of his teenage funk, how a mediocre student suddenly rose to the top of his class. All because he'd found his passion. But when my father made up his mind, there was little that could change it.

As fate would have it, Jason went to rabbinical school in New York. While he was there, he got to spend quality time with my father. One Sunday, my father called unexpectedly. "Delky, that boy of yours is so sweet and so smart; you have no idea!" I resisted the urge to say, "Even though he's Orthodox?" Because in spite of his biases, I truly adored my father.

He died the following year, but not before he came to love and accept his grandson. And every time I hear my son speak in public, I think, "My Daddy would be so proud!"

Where is my Home?

I've always had a recurring dream. The details have changed, but one thing is remains the same. I'm lost and can't find my way back home. In some of the dreams I try to punch in a phone number, but my fingers can't find the right keys. In one dream I tried to call 911. But when they asked my address, I got stuck. I couldn't remember where I lived.

When I'd wake up, I was usually shaking. And to be honest, the dreams were more frequent after an unexpected loss. Because grief can feel like you've ALWAYS been lost. But I've learned to shake it off. And it helps when I think of the special places that I used to call home.

The first was my childhood home on Long Island. My desk fit perfectly in the upstairs alcove, where I'd look out the window and dream about who I'd be when I grew up. My mother let me pick out the wallpaper. It was called Dancing Flowers, and swayed in the background as I sang out loud to my heart's content.

Childhood home in 1959. Nancy, Janet, Sydell

Being a young mother was another time when I felt at home. We lived in Diamond Bar, where everyone looked out for each other's kids. And that's how I found the Jewish community with our beloved Israeli rabbi. Once we connected with other young families, we all felt like we belonged.

But my house in Palos Verdes was the most fun. Remodeling that cute, fixer-upper was my favorite adventure with Rex, my set designer husband. The best part though, was watching my teenagers run in and out of that house: fussing with hair, dressing for prom, or just doing homework with friends. But mostly, I loved watching them blossom into miraculous young adults.

My kids are grown with homes of their own. And Rex has passed on. I wallowed around for a while. But then I woke up. After 27 years in PV, I sold my house and moved to the Westside. I still get scared when I dream about being lost, but I take a deep breath and try to move forward. Because when I make new connections, I start to feel at home.

So I remind myself of these truths:

We all get lost along the way, but then we get found.

When you lose someone you love, look for the open arms. They will be there to help you heal.

Because home is more than a place – it's where you choose to belong.

Sydell's childhood home on Long Island (Visiting in 2014)

High Holidays, Then and Now

Every year, for the Jewish High Holidays, I got three new dresses. My mother was always careful about money, but for the High Holidays, we splurged: two dresses for Rosh Hashanah and one for Yom Kippur. When we'd get home from shopping, I'd pull them all out, and she'd help me decide which to wear on which day.

My mother was tall and slim, with shiny dark hair and milky white skin. She was stylish too, so when she gave her opinion about what to wear, I knew I could trust her.

After temple, we usually had company over. My mother would plan for days and pull out all her favorite serving dishes. With little bits of white paper, she'd write the name of each food on the menu and put them carefully into the right serving dish. "What a clever idea," I thought. "She's so organized and has everything under control."

Nancy, Janet and Sydell, 1950

My life had order as a child, and I always knew what to expect. My mother had lots of rules, but they made me feel safe, and life was predictable… until the mood shifted in my house, and my mother began spending more and more time in bed. My father, always the joker, developed a cheerful façade. But I'd catch him sometimes when he didn't think I was looking and saw cracks in his smile that looked like worry.

I sensed something was wrong, but when I asked my father, he said, "No, sweetheart, everything's fine." My mother was no longer able to cook dinner, so my 16-year-old sister Nancy became the designated cook. I was 13, and since I was never summoned to help, I watched and wondered. "Put the water on a high flame until it boils," I remember my mother shouting from the bedroom. "What do I do when it boils?" Nancy would shout back. "Lower the flame and add 1 cup of rice. The measuring cups are to the right of the sink."

My mother died that May, and it was the end of my three new holiday dresses. Instead of having celebrations at home, we started going to my Aunt Ruth's for Rosh Hashanah. My father was still pretending to be cheerful, so I learned the skill and joined in the game. It was the only way to earn his favor, so I tried my best to laugh with all the relatives. But when I got home, I'd go up to my room and close the door.

At home, my father could no longer pretend, and I began to see through it. He was sad and quieter around the house, and like me, he spent more time alone. Nancy was away at nursing school. I was alone in my room, and my father was downstairs, alone in his.

Jason, Sydell & Emily 2018

We didn't have a word for it then, but I can see now that both my father and I were depressed. I carried around my inner loneliness like a child carrying a backpack that's too heavy to hold. But I had no choice; the wound was too deep, and I was taught to keep it inside. It was the only way to not upset the grownups in my orbit.

It's over 50 years later, and the High Holidays are different for me now. My son, who was ADHD before it was popular to diagnose, was never interested in services at temple. My daughter would sing all the prayers out loud by my side, but Jason would fidget and beg to go outside and play. "Will he ever get what the High Holidays are about?" I used to think. But every year, I took him to temple anyway and never gave in to his pleas to stay home.

This year, I bought myself three new outfits for the High Holidays. Sunday, I tried them all on and decided by myself which one I should wear to each service. On Monday morning, I put on my new black and white polka dot top with a flowy black skirt. Fortunately, it was cool, so I was able to add the new linen jacket I bought to go with it. I was meeting friends, so I was excited about going to services.

I walk into the auditorium, now turned sanctuary, and take a seat in the reserved section where my friends are sitting. There is a joyful mood all around. After all, Rosh Hashanah is the Jewish New Year, a happy day for celebration. The rabbi walks in, and my head turns. He is a nice-looking man of about 40, with flecks of grey in his beard. He is smiling and laughing and greeting the many people he knows and loves.

He begins the service with a story – a joke, actually – about "Shtisel," the Netflix series about a religious family in Israel. The congregation is laughing and enjoying his sense of humor. I turn to my girlfriend, whom I've known for almost 40 years. "Can you believe that is Jason?" I ask. "I know," she replies. "Unbelievable!"

Jason is my son, and here he is with 500 people, leading the prayers, making jokes, and sharing his insights about Judaism with the rest of the congregation. He is the senior rabbi at Cedars-Sinai Medical Center, and he's channeling my father's Milton Berle humor, gratefully updated for 2019. Two of his children are sitting behind me, looking attentive and adorable. Ayden is ten, and Koby is 12 and a half, almost a bar mitzvah.

I take it all in, remembering the holidays from my childhood perspective. It would take my mother's breath away to see this grandson she never got to meet. And what "naches" she'd get from seeing two of his five children sitting right here in their new holiday outfits. My father would also be proud – not just because Jason is a rabbi, but also because he exudes that Horowitz charisma and unflinching sense of humor.

Life goes on, and seasons change. A lonely girl grows up and has a family of her own. Heartaches come and go as we learn to be resilient. Sadness resides in my soul, but I have found the courage to move forward. I have two grown children with beautiful families of their own. I am happy because this year, I am not alone. I am in a sanctuary surrounded by love.

Nancy

Having a big sister has always made me feel safe. Nancy and I shared the same room for ten years and hid the same family secrets.

When we couldn't sleep at night, we'd rub each other's backs as we counted to a hundred. When I was homesick at sleepaway camp, she was the one who listened to me cry and tried to console me. When my mother was sick, my sister did all the cooking as I watched her in awe. And when my mom died of cancer, it was Nancy who rounded up my friends and brought them over to make me feel better.

My sister is four years older than I am, and at 18 was tall enough to hear my father whisper, "Don't cry!" as we walked to our seats at my mother's funeral. Is that when she learned to keep her pain inside? I wish I knew. But when feelings aren't processed, they often show up in our bodies.

Sydell and Nancy Horowitz, 1950

Three months after our mother died, my sister went away to nursing school. Within six weeks, she came down with an intestinal flu, but was sure she had the same symptoms as my mother. After being hospitalized for a month, she had no choice but to drop out of school. She took a job, got married, and had her first child, all by the time she was 20.

But physical pain continued to follow her: a hysterectomy in her 30's, back surgery in her 40's, and neuropathy in her 50's. And in the past several years, she's had hip replacement, surgery on her hammer toes, and reconstruction of both her feet because of excruciating pain from arthritis. She's never been in psychotherapy because she doesn't believe in it, but she keeps her spirits high. That is until the coronavirus hit.

Throughout this period of isolation, Nancy has been experiencing enormous amounts of physical pain. Her hip hurt, and then her back acted up. She risked going out so she could get shots for the pain and drugs to calm her down. Oxycodone, valium, Percocet, the works. We all love her, but it's come to a point where I'm almost irritated by her complaints. "Here we go again, another pain issue from Nancy."

A week ago Saturday, my sister was not feeling well. She lives in Florida and called one of her daughters, who lives nearby. She had thrown up and had abdominal pain. My niece insisted she call an ambulance and get herself to the emergency room. By the time Nancy arrived, she had sepsis, and by the evening, it turned into septic shock.

They rushed her to surgery, looking for an obstruction in her colon, but the bowel had improved, so they closed her back up. Then, they found a kidney infection and E. coli bacteria in her blood. It's been 11 days, and her white blood count is still high, her kidneys aren't producing urine, and her fingers and toes have turned purple and might not be salvaged.

My sister is the first one I call when I'm upset, when I don't know what to do, when I'm angry at someone I love. She listens, and if she responds in a way I don't like, I can yell at her without risking her love. But now I am worried. I'm worried that I might lose her from the aftereffects of septic shock. And I'd be lost without my big sister, the one who nurtured my soul and connects me to my roots.

Nancy and Sydell outside our home, 1962

Dear God, Please don't let her die! Nancy is my home, my safe place, my first childhood friend. I take a deep breath and send it out to Florida. "I love you, Nanny. Please get well!"

Hands and Feet

I lather shampoo into my hair, using my fingernails to massage my scalp. As I step out of the shower, I bend my neck forward so I can wrap a towel, turban-style, around my wet hair. I head to my bedroom, where I plug in the blow dryer with one hand and grab a round brush with the other. My hair sufficiently dry, I zip up my jeans, lace my sneakers, snap on my dog's leash, and take Sammy for a walk.

Simple movements that I barely used to notice are now in sharp focus. Activities that my sister Nancy will never again get to enjoy. Last Wednesday, June 24, she had her feet and hands amputated. How could this happen to a previously healthy woman? Covid made my world feel unsafe, but now I'm in absolute turmoil.

Nancy and Sydell February 2022

My sister had a kidney infection that went undiagnosed. She thought she had back pain, but it was a simple UTI. She took some painkillers and tried to sleep it off. But the infection turned to sepsis, and by the time she got to the hospital, it became septic shock. All her organs began shutting down. They worked for weeks to get them functioning, but the blood flow to her extremities never came back.

My sister has been living in Florida for over 30 years, and although her family lives nearby, they can't go and see her during the pandemic. I keep getting secondhand reports. I spoke to her by phone yesterday, but I'm in shock. Not septic shock, fortunately, but emotional disbelief. If it can happen to my sister, it could happen to me, especially since I live alone.

I'm flooded with fear and anxiety. Images of my sister lying helpless in a hospital bed with no hands or feet repeat on a continuous loop in my head. What would I do if something like that happened to me? My sister had a choice; she would have died without the amputations. At 77, she chose life. I'm not sure I would have made the same choice.

A life without privacy would be too much to bear. To give up the freedom to wash my own hair, fix my own coffee, feed myself, and go to the bathroom alone is unfathomable. I'd rather count my blessings, cut my losses, and peacefully let go. Or so I think.

Three years have passed since her surgery, and my sister is doing well. She has prosthetics from her knees down and gets around with a walker. With the two half fingers on her left hand, she can make her own coffee, put a key in the door, and manage her cell phone. My sister has made friends at her senior residence, and her husband is by her side. At 81 years old, she has a positive attitude and continues to play bridge.

Nancy has become an inspiration to those who know her because she's made peace with her life and enjoys what she has. I'm proud of my sister Nancy, and I love her to bits!

My Stepmother's Funeral

I ride to the cemetery with my stepsister's daughter, a red-headed beauty who always makes me feel included. My stepbrother's daughter is sitting in the back with her husband, and they are all sharing memories. Their beloved grandmother passed away two days ago, and although she was 90 years old, it was still sudden and unexpected.

She was my stepmother, and I loved her. Lila was married to my father for 36 years, and we had a warm relationship, even after my father died 15 years ago. But I live in California, and I never really thought of her as a mother.

Sydell & Lila, 2006

My real mother died when I was 14. My father remarried a few years later. He then sold our home, and we moved in with her family. She had also been widowed, but her children adored my dad. The bond grew stronger as my stepsiblings got married and had kids of their own. He loved the grandchildren and took pride in caring for their emotional and financial needs.

When we get to the cemetery, we stop at the mortuary to see if my stepsister and her husband have arrived. It's hot and muggy, and my hair is starting to frizz like it used to when I lived in New York. I feel like such an outsider among this group of step-relatives. But they were my father's family, and I've come to pay my respects.

As soon we get to the burial site, I look for my mother's grave. She is buried next to my father. And now my stepmother will be buried on my father's other side. Lila's first husband is also buried in this family plot, and she'll be placed between the two of them. I know, one big happy family.

I leave the group of mourners to look for my mother's gravestone. But all I can see is a large pile of dirt that's been dug up in preparation for the new grave. I brush the orange clay dirt away with my fingertips, and slowly, my mother's gravestone is revealed: "Janet Horowitz, Beloved Wife, and Mother." But I see what's etched in my mind instead. "Janet Horowitz, forgotten by her husband, forsaken by her daughters who never learned to talk about her or grieve for her loss."

And once again, I become that lonely girl of 14, looking down at my mother's grave in utter disbelief. "Mommy, why did you leave me? Why did I have to struggle alone while they got to have Daddy? Why did Lila get 90 years when you only got 44?"

My heart is broken, but I dig up a stone from the ground and put it on my mother's grave to let her know I was here. "I love you, Mommy. I love you." With tears in my eyes, I join the other mourners to honor my stepmother, the love of my father's life.

Chapter Three

Love and Loss

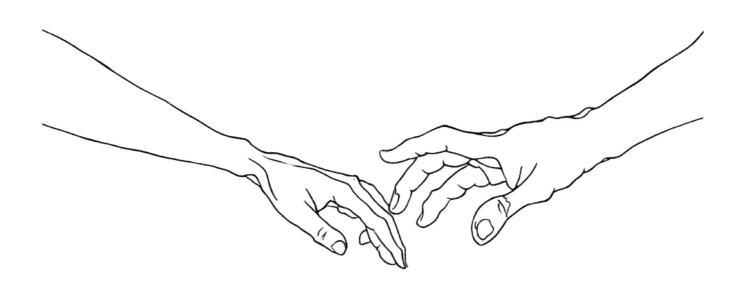

Enchanted Collaboration

As a director of theatre, I have always appreciated the art of collaboration. Besides working with actors, I brought together set, lighting, and costume designers. When creative artists are open and feed off each other's ideas, we do our best work. But at Cal State Dominguez Hills, I experienced an enchanted collaboration.

I was nervous about directing *A Midsummer Night's Dream* since it was my first Shakespeare on a college campus. Would my students be able to handle the language well enough for the audience to understand? It was a three-and-a-half-hour play, so when I found a cutting that brought it down to a manageable two hours, my doubts began to subside.

Sydell Rex, September 3, 1992

I started by meeting with Rex, Cal State's hot shot set designer. He strutted into the green room wearing his usual paint-covered jeans and a wad of keys hanging from his belt loop.

He was an intense, wiry man in his mid-40s who was passionate about his work. We'd already done a few shows together, so I wasn't intimidated. We agreed to have an initial design meeting after he'd read through my cut version of the script.

I came to his office the following week bearing two cups of high-octane coffee, the kind found in every theatre department. I was relieved that he liked the cutting, which he affectionately referred to as the "Reader's Digest" version. "What image does the play evoke in you?" he asked. The question threw me for a loop. I was used to being asked, "Where do you want the entrance, downright or down left?" I'd never considered the idea of an image or an overriding concept. But it was the basis for our collaboration.

Rex 1990

I told him that my favorite part of A Midsummer Night's Dream was the fantasy of being in an enchanted forest with no rules or boundaries. My strongest image was of dreamlike characters flying free. He nodded and said, "Let me think about it." He came back to me the next day, this time bringing coffee to my office. On a piece of poster board he had painted a beautiful pink, yellow, and pale blue butterfly. "Does this say it to you?" he asked.

I loved the image, but it felt too literal. The play tells the story of star-crossed lovers who run away to a magical forest, where they're surrounded by creatures of the night.

"I see mysterious beings appearing unexpectedly from hidden caves and pathways," I told him.

"Would you like a darker, wilder atmosphere?" he asked.

"Exactly," I answered. "The butterfly just seems too tame."

"Yes, I see what you mean," Rex replied. "If we're true to the text, the fairies appear when night is at its darkest. I don't think I could create that with lighting effects alone."

I thought not but needed his input to be sure.

"Can you give the set a moodier, more romantic quality?" I asked. "It should reflect the forbidden love story of the mortals as well."

He smiled at me and nodded, letting me know we were on the same page. I was excited by how easily we could share our ideas and develop a concept just through conversation.

Three days later, Rex came back to me with an entire set design. The pinks and yellows had been replaced by deep purples and blues. His rendering looked like a roller coaster covered with iridescent pieces of delicate fabric.

50

There were places under rocks where the fairies could hide, appear, and then reappear somewhere else. Up left, ten feet off the ground, there was an asymmetrical stairway leading gradually down to center stage. This is where Oberon and his Queen Tatiana would make their stately entrances. I couldn't believe that this was the result of our collaboration.

A Midsummer Night's Dream

It was magical and inspired me to take chances as a director. With so many levels and hiding places, it seemed obvious to make the production more visual. The fairies pranced seamlessly from level to level. It looked like they were actually flying. The actors created stage pictures, and they enhanced the meaning of the play. If the audience didn't catch every word, they could easily understand by following the characters' movements. Instead of the words being obstacles, they became doors to visual images that opened everyone's imagination.

One night during the last week of rehearsals, Rex noticed how the actors seemed to populate every inch of his set. He leaned over to me, and I felt his breath close to my ear. "Sydell," he whispered, "you have a wonderful sense of composition." It was the sexiest thing anyone had ever said to me. By the end of A Midsummer Night's Dream, it was clear: I was in love with my set designer, and he was smitten

Sydell and Rex in 2013

51

with me.

Rex and I acknowledged our feelings for each other and decided to go on a date. It didn't take long for the artistic collaboration to turn deeply personal. In 1992, with all our friends and family present, we got married in our beautiful backyard. In the 30 years we have known each other, we have done over 20 productions together. But none of them compared to the richness of our 24-year marriage. I lost Rex two years ago, and I miss him terribly.

We had a lot of challenges, but I wouldn't have traded those years for all the enchanted forests of Shakespeare's boundless imagination.

Caution: Set Designer at Work

My husband Rex was a brilliant set designer. He did his best work in the scene shop behind the theatre at Cal State Dominguez Hills, where we worked together for 25 years.

The shop was 50 x 100 feet with 30-foot ceilings, and every inch had a designated purpose. There was a long workbench along the north wall with power saws spinning and the smell of sawdust everywhere. To me, it sounded like a dentist's office, but to Rex, it was wonderland, and he was in his glory. He was proud to be working with students and helping them build the sets he'd designed.

Our Town backdrop

When a set was all put together, I'd find him alone on stage, hanging from a cherry picker to touch up the paint.

I loved coming into the shop to check on a set for a show I was directing. I'd call out his name, and my voice would echo in the large concrete room. When he saw me, Rex's face would light up. He'd always stop what he was doing and take a break. We'd go outside to catch up on our day, laugh about the students who were driving us nuts, and enjoy a high-octane cup of coffee. Soon, he'd go back to work and get lost again in the thing he loved more than anything in the world.

It was fascinating to watch Rex work, especially when he was painting a backdrop. There was a paint frame along the east wall of the shop. He hung the muslin for

Here's To Love

53

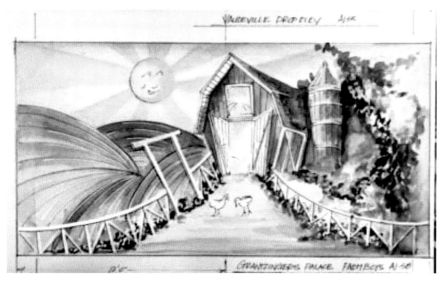

Gypsy: Farm Boys drop

his drop along the top of the frame. With a push of a button, the frame would go up so he could reach the bottom with his brush. With another push of the button, the frame went down so he could paint along the top.

He usually had students working the paint frame. They loved watching him transform a piece of muslin into a masterpiece. It could be the skyline of New York for *Guys and Dolls*, a sunny field with bales of hay for *Oklahoma*, or a quaint New England village complete with church and steeple for our favorite, *Our Town*.

I was one of the few who knew his secret weapon. Rex used a spray gun to create highlights and shadows. He used it with the focus of an orchestra conductor. He'd draw an outline of the scenery on the canvas while a student mixed paint at the sink near the frame. Then he'd lay in the details, grab his gun, and off he'd go. My husband was John Wayne of the paint frame, spraying in subtleties of color like he was waving a magic wand.

Rex was a genius; there's no argument there. His need to create beautiful art was unrelenting. But like most geniuses, he had little concern for his own well-being while he was working. The hours he spent spraying paint on canvas without a mask are too numerous to recount. And in the early days, he'd have a cigarette in his hand at the same time. Spray–breathe in fumes, spray–breathe in cigarette smoke, spray–and create phenomenal art.

My husband's work was astonishing, but he could have lived so much longer if he wasn't so reckless with his

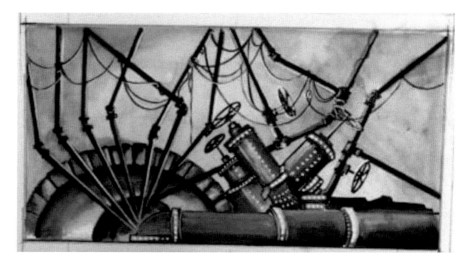

Guys and Dolls

54

health. Was that the madness of an artistic genius? I knew I was talented, but I was jealous of Rex's genius. Maybe I was lucky to be spared. As the saying goes, "Talent does what it can, and genius does what it must."

And now you are gone, my love, and I am alone. I'm angry and sad, and I miss you every single day.

Guys and Dolls: Sewer drop

I Remember

I remember standing at the top of the hill, ocean waves flirting with steep cliffs below.

You put your arm around me and with your other pointed ahead.

"There… that's where we're going to live, darlin'."

I remember dinner with all the kids and their friends. Everyone laughing and carrying on,

as we sat at our solid oak table in Lunada Bay.

I remember how you looked at me with love, when I had a problem and needed to talk.

It was your eyes, those deep, blue eyes. They held a gentle knowing

of who I was and what I needed to hear.

I remember the shame when you started drinking again.

Your 2nd DUI, your broken nose, your truck wrecked and in ruins.

I thought I'd lost you for good, but you came back and regained your sobriety.

I remember how helpless you looked when your body collapsed on our bedroom floor.

You cried out for help, but I couldn't get you up and didn't know what to do.

I called 9-1-1. It was 4 a.m. You were rushed to the hospital in a screaming red van.

I remember the doctor's voice on the phone when she matter-of-factly said,

"It's cancer, Sydell. He doesn't have long to live."

I remember hearing your rattled breathing turn to short, uneven gulps.

And then it turned quiet. I stared as you took your last breath.

I felt numb. Numb and alone and scared out of my mind.

I remember.

Rex in 2016

Surviving Complicated Grief

The hospital smells of disinfectant, trying to mask the presence of illness and grief. I walk into my husband's room and give him a hug. I hold on tight, and even though he's too weak to reciprocate, I relish the familiar touch and feel of his skin. How, I wonder, will I find the strength to witness his decline? He promised he'd never leave me, that he'd love me forever. But now he has cancer, and promises are a thing of the past.

Six weeks later, my sweet husband, Rex, passes peacefully at home. Even though I'm with him when he takes his last breath, I just stare in disbelief. Grief takes on many forms, and for now, I feel like I'm watching a scene in a really bad play. I walk through the funeral, burial, and

Rex in 1992 and 2016

reception like I'm a robot. I engage in conversation, but I'm not really present. There's a blanket between me and the rest of the world, and nothing's getting through.

When the feelings start to come, they are complicated and not what I expected. The anger kicks in first. I tear through Rex's tools and start packing them away. When I find corroded duplicates, I go to the dump and toss them out frantically. I call in a friend to take down the walls of his makeshift office in the garage. I clean out the space with a vengeance, furious at the mess he left behind. If I'm going to be alone, then I'll do what I want, so don't get in my way.

My kids are adults with families of their own, and I don't want to burden them unnecessarily. But toughing it out on my own is harder than I thought. Out of nowhere, with Rex gone six weeks, the tears start to come. They come to the supermarket when I can't decide between peaches and plums. They come when the light turns red, and I'm going to be five minutes late. And again, when the gas tank hits empty, and I've forgotten to fill it up. They come flooding when the dishes pile up in the sink, and the dishwasher is full. It doesn't take much, but for the next eight months, grief feels like it's never going to end.

When the fear kicks in, I suddenly feel very old. How will I navigate this next phase of my life on my own? Will I be lonely for the rest of my days? What if I get in an accident, and nobody knows about it until it's too late? Will I have enough money to live comfortably if I need long-term care? Who can I talk to when I'm feeling worried or sad, or happy and excited? Rex was my heart, the one I shared everything with, and now I have no idea where I'm supposed to turn.

I'm independent to a fault and resist reaching out until I see a card from The Gathering Place. They are offering a "Loss of Spouse" grief support group. Even though I'm not ready, it's close to my home, so I give it a chance. I go to the group for nine weeks and start connecting with other women. I start to make friends and surround myself with people who understand. "How did you deal with Social Security?" "Do you have to take your husband's name off the mortgage to set up a trust?" "What are you doing with his clothes?" "Who do you talk to when you are feeling hopeless?" And most importantly, "Tell me about your husband. What was he like?"

It's been three years since I lost the love of my life, and although I'm still grieving, I am beginning to have hope. I journal every morning to stay in touch with my feelings. I honor my husband by sending him loving prayers throughout the day. I've learned to reach out and ask for help when I need it. I know who I can really talk to and who just wants me to move on. But mostly, I've learned that I have not been abandoned. I have been loved and cherished by a man I adored, and that love gives me the strength to make it on my own.

Unexpected Acts of Kindness

"In a world where you can be anything, be kind." This quote is getting thousands of "Likes" on Facebook, but do we practice acts of kindness in our everyday lives?

In March of 2002, my husband Rex and I move to a small fixer-upper in Palos Verdes. Our next-door neighbor is a single guy named Mark. He is barely 30 and, like Rex, enjoys schmoozing in the driveway about home improvement. Rex invites Mark to one of his plays at the university, and that's where we meet his fiancée, Karen. They get married, Karen moves in next door, and before long, they're raising a family. No matter how busy they get, they remain our "go-to" neighbors when we go on vacation or need a favor.

As their children begin to grow, my husband's health begins to decline. At first, it's almost imperceptible, but as the years progress, he becomes increasingly tired with bouts of confusion. On an ordinary day in January 2014, I drove to the Westside to babysit my son and daughter-in-law's four kids. As soon as they leave for their "date," I get an urgent call on my cell phone.

Sydell & Rex 2002

"Rex is in his car in the driveway," my neighbor Karen says. "The car alarm is going off, and he's just sitting there, staring into space."

I'm with four kids under 10, and even if I could leave them, it would take me an hour and a half to get home in traffic. I tell her I'll call her back and start making some calls. Meanwhile, Karen brings Rex into my house and manages to turn off the car alarm. Her kids come over, too, because Mark isn't home, and they're too young to be alone. Fortunately, I reached my stepdaughter, who agreed to drive from Burbank and stay with her dad until I got home.

By the time I get there, Rex is running a high fever. I called 911, and he was taken by ambulance to Torrance Memorial Hospital. Everything happens fast, and before I know it, he's having his gallbladder removed. The doctor-on-call tells me not to worry; everything else checks out fine, and he'll be ready to go home in a few days. Even though he's given a clean bill of health, as I reflect on it now, it was the beginning of the end.

On July 28th, 2016, Rex took another emergency trip to Torrance Memorial. This time, I have my own doctor involved, and she personally runs all the tests that should have been

run in 2014. By noon the next day, we have a diagnosis: Stage 4 Bone Cancer. We do surgery, we do radiation, we do everything possible. But on September 17th, 2016, my sweet husband died in a hospital bed at home, and none of us knew what hit us.

With all the funeral arrangements and commotion in our family, I forget to tell Karen and Mark. About three weeks go by when Karen knocks on my door to ask about Rex. "Oh Karen, I'm so sorry I didn't tell you. He passed away three weeks ago." She stands on my doorstep as tears start flooding her eyes. "We loved him," she sobs. "Mark is going to be devastated."

The next few months go by in a blur. I do all the household chores and try to keep it together. I continue going to my daughter's house in Costa Mesa on Mondays to watch her kids. On those days, I don't get home until after 7 pm. Monday is garbage day, so I try to get the cans out on Sunday nights.

One Monday night, when I got home, I noticed that my empty cans had already been taken in. The neighbors on my other side were also very helpful when Rex was sick, so maybe it was them. Oh wait, I'm close to the rabbi who lives around the corner, so it could have been him. I have no idea who my "Secret Angel" is, and I want to find out so I can thank them.

The next Monday night, as I was driving home, I saw Mark and his 10-year-old son Bobby in front of my house. They're wheeling my garbage cans to the sideyard. I roll down my car window and call out, "Are you the one who's been doing this for the past few weeks? He looks like a kid with his hand caught in the cookie jar. "We try to," he answers sheepishly; "it's no big deal."

The next day I see him alone in his driveway and go over. "Thank you so much, Mark," I say. "You don't have to do this every week, really." He smiles at me with a look of embarrassment and says, "I want Bobby to learn about neighbors and chores. And besides," he pauses with a catch in his throat, "I loved Rex. I want to do this for him."

That was a year ago, and they still take out my garbage on Sunday nights and return the cans on Monday without saying a word. A few months ago, when the fog in my brain started to lift, I bought Bobby a junior-size football that he freely retrieves from my backyard whenever it goes over the fence. For Thanksgiving, I made them all a huge gift basket with gummy bears and other kid-friendly treats. They're always appreciative, but they don't need gifts or recognition. Their acts of kindness seem to be helping them as much as it does me.

A few weeks ago, I knocked on their door because an unfamiliar car was blocking my driveway. When Karen answered, one of her friends heard me and apologized profusely. "I was just dropping off my kids; I'll move my car in a second." I started chatting with Bobby and his 9-year-old sister Julie. We're laughing about our dogs digging under the fence so they can play together. Julie is very talkative, and I'm enjoying the friendly banter with my next-door neighbors' kids.

A few days later, I got home from work feeling tired and cranky. As I approach my front door, I see a pink gift bag with ribbons overflowing. Inside, there is a handmade card, and on the front, it says: "A little Gift for…" I open it, and it says, "YOU! Look in this bag! I made this for you!! Love, Julie!" I rummage through the bag, and I find it: a 2-inch-wide heart made from over 30 pink beads. It's adorable! This 9-year-old child's gesture has touched me beyond words.

It's easy to resort to self-pity when you lose someone you love. Believe me, I've done more than my share. Yet, who would have thought that the single guy next door would morph into this beautiful, loving family? Their unexpected acts of kindness have been instrumental in helping to lift my spirits.

They make me think of all the other caring people who've been there for me since I lost my husband. I am so grateful. Acts of kindness remind us of our shared humanity. For the past year and a half, I've been the recipient, and now it is time to pay it forward. The greatest acts of kindness are helping others without expecting anything in return. In Hebrew, we call it a Mitzvah. And what better way to honor the memory of my dear husband, Rex.

I Used to Be Pretty

I used to be pretty--I mean cheerleader, actress, head-turning pretty. Fortunately, I was also smart. I learned early that it would take more than good looks to make my way in the world. And as much as I'm struggling with aging, it's harder for women whose identities revolved around their husbands, their children, and their fleeting good looks.

I always felt an urgency to craft a meaningful life. My mother died at 44, so I knew firsthand that life could be short. I calculated the most likely path to success and pursued a PhD According to plan, I secured a tenure-track position at a state university and thought I had it all figured out. Aging wasn't going to mess with me.

What I hadn't figured out was how older women are treated in our society. Granted, I live in Los Angeles, the land of the young and beautiful. But it seems to be pervasive; as women age, they are often dismissed as irrelevant. "What could you say that would interest me?" their critical eyes seem to say. Or if I take ten seconds too long at the checkout line, their carts inch up to the register while my groceries are still being bagged.

I didn't dwell on it when my husband and I were still working professors, but when we retired, it was hard to ignore. Our lives slowed down, and we enjoyed the time to just sit and have coffee, while everyone rushed around us.

Rex had a history of smoking and bouts of alcoholism, which aged him prematurely. He loved to go to Starbucks for a latte with whipped cream and a gooey French pastry. Since Rite Aid was only two stores away, stopping there before Starbucks became part of his daily routine.

Every day he'd pick up Band-Aids or shaving cream or toothpaste, or whatever single item game him an excuse to go to Rite Aid. He grew up working in the hayfields, so he never felt comfortable with the PhDs at the university. Going to Rite Aid became his way to connect with his "peeps." The clerks and checkout people all loved him, because he took the time to talk to them and often had them laughing in the aisles.

As my husband's health began to decline, so did his trips to Rite Aid. When I started picking up his medications, I was greeted with questions, advice, and many well wishes. I gave them constant updates, but when I told them he was on hospice, their pitying looks cut right through my core. Hospice delivered his medications at home, and I was frankly relieved that I no longer had to face his friends at Rite Aid.

On September 17, 2016, Rex died peacefully at home. Even though I was still in my 60s, I suddenly felt terribly old. My daughter and daughter-in-law sprang into action and took over all the arrangements. In Jewish law, the burial should take place soon after death, so there were a lot of preparations for the gathering at my house two days later. I appreciated the help of my beautiful girls, but I felt useless and extraneous as the activity swirled around me.

It was several months before I went back to Rite Aid for some prescriptions of my own. I was in sloppy clothes, with no make-up, and felt about ten years older. It broke my heart to tell his "peeps" that he had passed away. They all made sympathetic remarks and couldn't have been nicer. But something had changed. From that point on, they would always see me as "Rex's widow." The sad looks in their eyes made me want to run out screaming every time I bumped into someone he knew.

A few months later, I went to the pharmacy, looking worse than I had in my entire life. Yeah, grief has a way of doing that to you. I asked for my medications, hoping there would be someone at the counter who didn't know Rex. Of course, Linda was there, and she greeted me with those pitying eyes that seemed to say, "Oh, you poor pathetic creature, how hard it must be to be old and alone." I know I'm projecting because she was sweet as could be, but I'd gained 15 pounds and looked like hell.

Linda put my medications on the counter and instructed me to insert my card into the payment machine. The first screen came up. "Press the X in the right-hand corner," she told me before I had even read what was on the screen. As soon as the next screen came up, she blurted, "Check the box if you want a consultation." When the third screen came up, without even waiting a second, she instructed: "Sign on the bottom line and hit 'next.'"

This went on for several months. I know she meant well, but she prompted me on every screen before I could even read what it said. I started feeling nervous at the counter and afraid that I couldn't answer the simplest questions on my own. Was I just a feeble old lady who couldn't even handle an ATM machine? I'd finally had enough and had to speak up. "Are you treating me like this because of my age? I mean, give me a minute to read the screen, and I'm sure I can figure it out myself. Please have some respect!"

I grabbed my medications and stormed out of the store. I walked over to Starbucks, where it's quieter, and found a bench outside. What I really wanted to say was, "I used to be pretty! I have a PhD, and I can take care of myself! Don't you dare treat me like an old lady!" As I sat there feeling sorry for myself, the tears started to come. Maybe that's who I am to the rest of the world now, I thought as the tears grew more insistent.

I took a deep breath and felt a warm breeze blow over me. As I looked up, a dark cloud passed slowly in front of the sun. Just then, a blue and green bird perched on the back of my bench and made himself at home. I imagined what Rex would say if he were here with me. "It's O.K. darlin', I know this is hard, but you'll get through it. Just remember our love and give yourself time." And with that, the bird flew away as quickly as it had come, and the sky began to brighten.

It's two years later and I do feel better about myself. I've moved closer to my kids and grandkids, and I wear matching clothes when I go to the pharmacy. Although I'm aging like the rest of my generation, my mind is sharp, and my confidence is coming back.

Today, instead of turning heads, I counsel people who are struggling with relationships and feel overwhelmed by grief. When I'm not working, I go to the theatre, discuss world affairs, and spend time with my family and friends.

I was married to a man who knew me completely. To Rex, I was more than just pretty; I was smart and talented and the world's best director. When I could no longer see myself through his loving eyes, I got lost and let others define me.

Aging's not easy and neither is loss. But today, I have strength to slowly move forward with courage and hope. Rex would be proud.

Does the Soul Survive

I've always struggled with the concept of life after death. Does our soul live on in the minds and hearts of those we've touched? Can it exist separately in another dimension? If the soul survives, is it possible to communicate with a lost loved one? Can they come to us in times of need to give us comfort? Or when we die, is that it —over, finished, end of story?

Although I'm no stranger to existential dilemmas, it's been constantly on my mind since I lost my husband in 2016. I feel his spirit intensely throughout our home. We lived here together for 15 years, so naturally, there are many associations with the times we shared. But it's more than that.

Before I go to bed, I enjoy sitting in a dimly lit corner of my room. I sink into the big, cushy chair, and I'm comforted by its softness and warmth. I stay there as long as I can until I start nodding off. I'm afraid to get up and go to bed because I know what will happen. Once I take the eight steps across the room, I'll be wide awake. My husband's presence seems to grab onto me, and before I know it, I'm in the throes of anxiety.

The hardest time is falling asleep at night. I'm flooded with memories, and not all of them are good. A year into our marriage, he started drinking after seven years of sobriety. It was hard on my kids, who uprooted their lives when I remarried. I wanted to protect them, but his behavior was hard to defend. I began to lose confidence, not only in Rex but in the dream on which I had hung all my hopes. And the guilt follows me to bed.

Sydell & Rex in 1994

But even the good memories make me sad. We loved talking through the endless details of our day. We'd hold hands or swing a leg over the other, and the conversation was easy. Regardless of the issue, in bed we would listen and always be gentle with each other. It's where we felt closest and the most at ease.

I thought I could block out the pain if I made some changes to my room. I bought a new mattress and indulged in expensive bedding. I even put down a new carpet. But the second I sit on the new mattress, Rex is still there. I try my best to shut out the feelings and push them away, but he haunts me.

My friend Susan suggested I embrace his spirit and let my feelings in. She's right, of course. I just don't know how to do it.

I can keep most of my fears in check during the day, but in the darkness of night, they are magnified. What if I have a nightmare? Will it overwhelm me? If I get sick during the night, will I be able to take care of myself? I have people who love me, but when I'm alone in bed, I lose sight of that reality. Will I always be alone? What if I get a terminal illness? Will I linger and be a burden to my family, or will I be blessed with a peaceful death?

On difficult nights, I soothe myself by getting something to eat and bringing it to bed. I know full well that food won't do the trick, but old habits die hard. Sometimes, I stave off my fears by distracting myself with social media or reading a book. Whatever I do, I know it will take a while before I can settle down again and fall asleep.

Last night, as usual, I got up from my chair at the last possible moment. There is meditation music playing softly on my phone, and the house is quiet and warm. I walk across the room, and the familiar anxiety start to take hold. But instead of giving in to it, I turn off the light, get under the covers, and focus on the softness of my new, luxurious comforter.

I start to consciously slow my breathing and still my body. I relax my shoulders and neck to release the tension, and that's when I feel it. My eyes are closed, but I see a dark shadow cross over me. I know it is Rex, and for a moment, I feel him drifting away. I concentrate on him, and the dark shadow returns. As it envelops me, a light seems to pierce through. And for the first time in months, I started to feel calm.

It is Rex's spirit, I'm sure of it. But instead of chasing it away, I welcome it. I feel his love and embrace his spirit. I remember the deep connection we shared and the strength of our commitment to each other. He could always comfort me just by being near and joining with my deepest self—no judgement, no criticism, just acceptance and love.

I am finally able to understand my friend Susan's message. If I let him in, Rex will come to me when I need him the most. I don't have to run from the pain; I can learn to forgive. And I can still cherish the good parts and be warmed by his love.

I am beginning to do it more often, and it's starting to work. When I get into bed at night, I slow my breathing and try to calm myself. Then, I focus on a specific memory where we were deeply connected. I see it play out in my mind until I can feel his presence. And for those few precious moments, his soul provides me with comfort and healing.

I'm not sure if this is life after death, but my husband comes to me in the comfort of our bed. Will I be able to transform my fears and anxiety into peace and acceptance? I'm certainly trying. So when his soul reaches out to me, I will try to embrace it.

Rex's love was a blessing and an integral part of who I am. When I make peace with the past, I'm able to stay in the present – and that gives me hope for the future.

Vacationing as a Widow

Vacationing as a widow changed my perspective. Do relationships look the same on land and at sea? I'm on a cruise with my sister and brother-in-law, and as much as I love them, it's my first vacation without my husband. My sweet Rex died a year and a half ago, and I am still trying to navigate the seas… pun intended.

A pretty blonde on Deck 5 leans across the bistro table and smiles at her husband. She notices that his coffee is darker than usual and whispers, "Do you need more milk for your coffee?" He smiles back and looks deeply into her eyes. "Thanks, babe, that would be great!" They are in their 20s and obviously in love. The gentle way they speak to each other reminds me of the sweetness that defined my marriage. Rex never raised his voice to me and always made sure I had everything I needed.

Two tables over, a 40-something couple in bright red tee shirts engage in an animated conversation. A teen-aged girl with a thick brown ponytail runs over to their table. Another girl, her sister maybe, joins her, and together they begin their appeal. "Mom, can we pleeeeese have money for ice cream?" After some playful banter and a lot of laughing, the girls run off to purchase their treats.

I have two grown children, so the days of them begging for ice cream money are long gone. Fortunately, my kids are self-supporting with jobs, homes, and families of their own. I'm proud of them and love my beautiful grandchildren. As I watch this family, I long for the day when my kids needed me that way. I'm fine on my own, but how nice it would be to put extra milk in my husband's coffee.

As I start feeling sorry for myself, an older man passes by, pushing his wife in a wheelchair. Just then, my focus shifts to a 50ish-year-old woman as she grabs

Nancy and Sydell on a cruise, December 2017

her husband's hand on the steps so she doesn't lose her footing. Yes, cruising is for couples, and I'm grateful for the chance to be spending quality time with my sister and brother-in-law. And yet, as I watch all the couples stroll by, I am once again hit with the reality of being a widow. I'm trying to have a good time, when suddenly the tears come uninvited.

I've been a couple for so long that it feels like I'm missing a limb. I know the "rules" for being married, I just don't know how to behave as a widow. Will I just get used to being alone? Or will I tag along with married friends and relatives on their vacations? Maybe I'll find girlfriends to travel with. Or would it be easier to just stay home to avoid the discomfort? I decide to call it a day and go to my cabin to indulge in a little pity party.

Fortunately, by the next morning, my attitude had improved. I drag myself out of bed and go for coffee on the Promenade Deck. To my right, I hear a 70ish-year-old woman with dyed orange hair berating her husband. Her voice is loud and shrill. "Didn't you go to the bathroom?" she scolds. "I told you to go before we left the room. You'll never find a clean toilet in port! Why don't you ever listen to me?" He doesn't look embarrassed; he's apparently used to this, so I simply look away

We get off the ship in Aruba and an overweight man in his 60s shouts across the gangway to his wife. "It's too slippery; I can't do these steps," he yells. "That's not my fault," she retorts, "If you lost weight like you're supposed to, it wouldn't be a problem!" She eventually goes over to him and helps him down the steps. "I knew this cruise wasn't a good idea," I hear her complain under her breath.

Marriage isn't perfect; I understand that firsthand. Rex and I certainly had our share of problems. My first year as a widow, I was angry all the time (in between bouts of depression). Now I'm remembering the good times, and probably idealizing them in the process. I long for his company when I have something on my mind that I'm burning to share. Talking things through with him always helped me make better sense of my feelings. I miss the easy way we could talk about our day, books we'd read, politics, theatre, and especially the people we loved. We had such fun going places at home or away, and I miss his company, his companionship, his loving eyes.

And yet, there are days when I'm almost comfortable being a widow. I can walk at my own pace and make my own decisions. I can stay up as late as I want, and I don't have to tiptoe when he's napping. Don't get me wrong, I miss him terribly, but I'm adjusting to being alone.

I am grateful that we had a loving marriage that thrived both on land and at sea. I will always love you, Rex; nothing could ever change that. I'm just starting to hear my own voice and walk my own path. And with that comes a new freedom that I'm actually starting to enjoy. Thank you, Rex, for giving me the courage to enter this next phase of my life alone.

I Miss Those Years

"Mommy, can you sew a button on my P.E. uniform?" "Ma, I sat on my homework, and it's wrinkled, can you iron it?" "Mom, I signed you up to bring cookies on Thursday, OK?" These are the sounds that filled my home for over twenty years. There were so many things to do while I was going in so many different directions. They were frantic days, but they were filled with love and a sense of purpose.

My son was an active child, always testing the limits. He crashed toy trucks into walls, colored outside the lines, and was "all boy." Sometimes, when my eight-month-old puppy starts running around in circles, I call him my son's name by mistake. He reminds me of that playful boy who was full of the dickens. Without thinking, I repeat the phrase I used too often with my son: "What is your problem?!!" But to no avail.

My boy had a deep, sensitive side as well. I sang to him at night and read Dr. Seuss until I knew those books by heart. When he couldn't sleep and wanted to be near me, he'd sneak into my room and crawl under the bed. Dr. Spock had told us that co-sleeping was bad, and my son knew he'd be sent back to his room if he was caught. I wish I had followed my instincts and let him curl up in my arms and stay there all night.

My daughter Emily never lacked self-confidence. Although she got glasses at 15 months old and had bushy, Jewish hair, she thought she was the cutest thing on earth. She was a leader, with a trail of blonde-haired, blue-eyed girls following her every move.

When she decided to run for sixth-grade president, we practiced her speech night after night. She walked confidently onto the stage, looking like a ten-year-old Ruth Bader Ginsburg. I mouthed every word with her as

Sydell & Jason 1986

Emily 1983 & 2018

she gave her speech, and when she won, I said, "Today, sixth grade, tomorrow the world!" We laughed for days over that line.

When she was in seventh grade, we moved to Palos Verdes, and she was teased for the first time in her life. Some girls made fun of her glasses, and she came home that day in tears. I immediately made an appointment for her to get contact lenses. I urged her to leave the "mean girls" and find a nicer group of kids. She was smart enough to find her way through a difficult transition.

How I loved being at the center of my children's lives, being the one they came to for love and support. I remember watching my son play Little League and praying for a "ball" so he'd at least get on base. And what fun we had with my daughter's costume fittings for ballet recitals and bringing her roses backstage. I found such joy in watching my children's faces light up when I came home early from work. I was loved, I was needed, I was their mommy.

My house is quiet now. My husband died almost three years ago, and my children are out on their own. So I hold on tight to the memories.

My son is 40 and my daughter is 38. They have successful careers and children of their own. They have spouses who come first, as well they should. I know they love me, but the dynamics have changed. Instead of playing a leading role, I am now one of the supporting players.

Sydell with Jason and Emily, 1992

I've retired from my career as a college professor, and age is catching up with me. There are days when the loneliness overwhelms me. I'm up at 6 a.m. and sit on the couch until 10, waiting

Sydell with Jason & Emily, 2018

for a reason to get dressed and get out. There is nobody there to ask how I slept or keep me company while I make coffee and watch the news. Day after day, the monotony continues as I search for a new direction.

When I try to be grateful for all the good in my life, it actually makes me feel better. There are so many ways to reach others in similar situations. I am discovering a new freedom and enjoying getting involved in more social activities. Writing has become a new form of creative expression, and it's helping me find a new purpose.

Yes, I miss those years, but how fortunate I am to have had them. How fortunate to see my children thrive as adults and know that I had a big part in it. The future is not just theirs; it's mine, too. And it's time to move forward. I will welcome the next chapter of my life with courage, hope, and humility.

Moving to the Westside

It was the best of times; it was the worst of times. My son and daughter-in-law welcomed a fifth child into their family, and I just moved closer to them. My house in Palos Verdes has been on the market for more than five months, and last week, it fell out of escrow for the second time.

It was my safe zone, my nest egg, the keeper of memories that I shared with my late husband Rex. And now strangers are traipsing through and picking it apart. I'm counting on the equity to pay the expenses of the overpriced house I'm renting in Beverly Hills. So now I'm scared. Will I have enough until my house sells? Will I be enough to handle this? Am I strong enough to make it on my own?

Walking to Jason's house with Sammy, 2021. Sydell, Noa, Ely & Ayden

The house I'm renting is sweet, but it's unfamiliar. I don't know how to turn on the confection oven. The glass doors in the shower have sediment on them that won't come off. I'm sure they're more than 20 years old, and if I owned this house, I'd have them replaced. I turned on the heater in the pool Saturday, and now I can't figure out how to turn it off.

The landlord ordered a new dishwasher, and when it came two weeks ago, it was the wrong size. I have to wait another two weeks for the replacement. In the meantime, all I have is a big empty hole where the dishwasher belongs. It's the hole in my heart that opened when Rex died, and now it feels just a little more fragile. I'm used to doing things myself, but now I have to wait for the landlord in DC to talk to his mother three blocks away, and the right hand never knows what the left hand is doing.

And then, there's the fact that the HVAC system won't turn on. I wait again, and I'm promised a new motor this week. But it's cold at night, and I'm powerless to fix it on my own. It costs over a thousand dollars, and it's not my responsibility. I feel helpless, like the daze I was in when I lost my mother at 14 years old. I try to be brave, but all these changes are sometimes too much to bear.

I affectionately call it "Widow Shit." Losing a loved one is so much more than grieving the person you miss. It's figuring out how to spend your remaining years. It's moving away from a community you love because there's nothing there for older, single women. It's trying to navigate being a renter after 40 years of homeownership. It's learning your way around a new community where there's steep underground parking, even at Trader Joe's. What a cool adventure it would be, exploring a new community with Rex. We'd laugh at the underground garages and explore all the cafes together. I miss him beyond words and moving brings it back to the forefront.

And yet, there are indescribable perks. Moving closer to my son means surprise visits at 7 a.m. when he's doing his morning run. It's being a mile and a half from five of my grandchildren. It's my sweet daughter coming over with new beach towels and a lady-like tool kit to help me out. It's having my son's daughter telling my daughter that it's her turn to live near grandma. It's spur-of-the-moment pool parties in my backyard with the children and adults, all playing nicely together.

It's knowing that if I must go to the hospital, it would be Cedars, where my son is the manager of spiritual care, and I'd have excellent care.

I figured out the pool heater and called a repairman to show me how to work the confection oven. The new dishwasher is top-of-the-line, and the heat and air conditioning start working. I unpack in less than two weeks and hang my pictures on the walls. I reconnected with a dear friend and colleague who I never knew lived in this part of town. My house in PV sells, and I can relax about money.

It was the worst of times; it was the best of times. I've moved to the Westside and I'm settling in. And slowly finding ways to move forward with my life.

Michael

It was August of 2020, the sixth month of the pandemic. I was kept away from my grandchildren and social distanced from my kids. Every activity that gave my life meaning had been taken away: clients in my office, writing groups, concerts and lectures, book clubs and discussion groups, and live theatre with the intimacy of being physically present.

Sydell & Michael in Mexico 2021

I was lonely. It had been four years since my husband died, and I no longer had the distractions that kept me from wallowing in my grief. Something had to give.

So, one morning, feeling particularly brave, I went on Match.com. I wrote a profile, uploaded some pictures, and started to browse around.

After several clicks and a few conversations, I got a message from a man named Michael. We texted, we Zoomed, we talked, and finally set up an outdoor dinner date. We met at a restaurant that was a mile from my house, but to me, it felt like a journey to the other side of heartbreak.

I parked my car, flipped down the visor mirror, and made peace with the older version of myself. I took a deep breath and grabbed my phone.

"I just parked," I texted.

"I'm here," he wrote back.

Oh good. I wasn't the first to arrive.

"I'm wearing black, with a black and red scarf," I said.

"I'm naked," he shot back.

"It figures," I retorted, enjoying the banter.

So, with feigned confidence, I walked towards the restaurant. And then I saw him: a handsome man with a full head of thick silver hair. He waved, so I joined him at the outdoor table and removed my mask. "Hi, I'm Sydell." He smiled. "I'm Michael. You look just like your picture. Very pretty." I started to relax.

We talked about our careers. He was interested when I told him I was a theatre professor. "Who's your favorite playwright?" he asked. "Ibsen," I replied without hesitation. "I read an Ibsen play in college. A woman named Mrs. Alving with syphilis. Sound familiar?" "Of course," I answered. But for the life of me, I could not remember the name of the play.

He was in the restaurant business and let me in on the best place for eggplant parmesan. "I love eggplant," I gushed. "Oh good. I'll have to take you there," he told me.

Sydell & Michael 2021

A bottle of wine later, he returned me to my car. I drove to the ticket booth and got out my wallet to pay. The attendant grinned. "The gentleman behind you already paid." WOW… nice touch, Michael!

The next day, I searched like mad for the name of that Ibsen play. *Ghosts*, of course! "Oh well," I thought, "good excuse for a text."

"I remembered the name of that Ibsen play," I texted. "It's been bugging me." He answered immediately. "I'm getting under your skin. That's a good sign for a new relationship! Still want to go for that eggplant parmesan?"

On our second date, he brought eggplant parmesan to my backyard. He was charming and funny. His eyes lit up when he spoke, and when he smiled, his face seemed to glow. I immediately fell under his spell.

As the days and weeks passed, we became inseparable. We threw Yiddish expressions at each other, sang songs from old Broadway shows, lit candles every night, and danced down the aisle of the neighborhood Ralphs. We had the vacation of a lifetime in Zihuatanejo, with dinner under the stars three feet from the edge of the ocean.

One day, as I was rubbing his back, he started to smile. "My father used to pay me twenty-five cents to rub his back." I laughed. "My sister and I took turns with each other," I said. "But when it was my turn, she was always too tired."

We ate an early dinner and cozied up on the couch. His hand glided lazily on my back for what felt like an hour. When it stilled, he whispered, "That was for all the times your sister didn't rub your back." My jaw dropped. I was speechless.

I fell in love with his touch. But it was more than that. He knew how to listen and respond to my needs. It made me a better listener, and I also learned to become more responsive to him.

We always held hands. We held hands at night, and we held hands on the day that we got the diagnosis—esophageal cancer. I listened to the words, but they didn't compute. He was so strong and vital. We'd only been together for seven months. How could this be?

He had grown children who lived nearby, and I could have easily stepped back. But the initial PET scan showed that it had not spread, so with love and optimism, I stayed by his side. We found a house to rent, moved in together, and hoped for the best.

Caring for Michael became my mission in life—and I embraced it. We went back and forth to doctors' appointments, in and out of the hospital for tests and procedures, chemo, and radiation. I was always sure he'd get better, so I never gave up.

When he was hurting, I held him close and gave him love. And he returned that love in spades when he was healthy and even when he was so sick that he could barely speak. But after 13 months of treatment, his body finally gave out. On June 4, 2022, my dear Michael passed away.

I was devastated. How could this happen again? I didn't know how I'd go on. But slowly, ever so slowly, I came back to life. And when the tears began to dry up, I was grateful. l had found the courage to love again.

We all want things to last forever, but at my age, you realize that nothing really does. And that's O.K.

I had almost two years with this delicious, exuberant man. How could I ever be sorry for that?

Rest well, Michael, and thank you for coming into my life.

The Rain of Tears

The rain keeps falling like tears that won't let up. It's July 2016, my husband's birthday, but we go to bed early. Just before midnight, he gets up to go to the bathroom. On his way back, he falls in a heap on the floor. I try to help him, but he's too heavy to lift.

Palos Verdes is a beautiful, sleepy town with very little crime. So, when I call 9-1-1, help appears immediately. My bedroom is filled with six paramedics who look like they're from Chippendales. They get Rex off the floor and back to bed. His vitals are good, so they leave with well wishes.

Michael in 2021

We go back to sleep, relieved, but at 4 a.m., I hear Rex calling from the floor near the bathroom. He has fallen again. I'm so tired; I almost ask if I can just put a blanket on him and wait until morning. But he's hurting, so I call 9-1-1 again. This time, they take him out on a stretcher and rush him to the hospital.

Six weeks later, he's gone.

Fast forward five years. Michael has just started chemo, and he's not doing well. At 2 a.m., he gets out of bed and collapses on the floor. Unfortunately, I know just what to do. I call 9-1-1, and my bedroom in Beverly Hills is filled with paramedics. They're not as fast as PV, but they're just as hunky.

They take Michael's vitals, and since they're fine, they put him back to bed and leave. But in the morning, he is too weak to get up. So, I called 9-1-1 again, but this time, I contacted his doctor, who insisted he go to the hospital.

And like déjà vu, another man I love is taken away on a stretcher. Michael fights for another year, but he passes peacefully on June 4, 2022.

So, I ask the rain, "How much grief is enough? When will the sun come out and release me from these tears?" Please, 2023, please be a better year!

Chapter Four

Reflections

Recurring Themes

When my mother was diagnosed in 1956, Breast Cancer was whispered about as a shameful, messy women's disease. On the day she died, her mother and sisters cried, and my father was comforted by his parents, and I was left hugging the wall outside her room. It was 1961, the days of "children should be seen and not heard."

Since that time, there has been important research on the effects of early mother loss on relationships. There have also been studies on intergenerational trauma. Jewish immigrants from Eastern Europe in the early 1900s were escaping religious persecution. They often left elderly parents behind, who were unable to make the journey. They came with little money and were unable to speak the language.

My maternal grandmother was married off at 17 and separated from her sisters. She lost two babies before my mother was born, with little emotional support. The focus was on economic survival, and feelings took second place. From that perspective, I can better understand why my mother was rarely affectionate towards me.

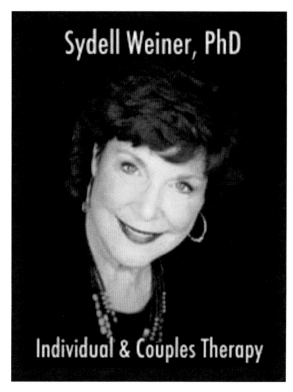

Sydell's Therapy Website, 2014

But some of her distance was probably a result of her illness. And since it was kept secret, I took it personally and wondered what I'd done wrong. Maybe it was comments like "How could you be so stupid?" or "Sorry isn't good enough." Maybe it was the spankings or washing my mouth out with soap, but I remember her disapproval more than I remember her love.

I have come to realize that the critical voice in my head that scolds me when I do something wrong is a distorted memory of my mother. Even though I yelled at my daughter when she was growing up, we got to have an adult relationship and work it out. With my mother gone by the time I was 14, we never had that option. So when the voice in my head blames me for something that's not my fault, I have to pause and remind myself that even if I am at fault, I am still worthy of love.

But more than losing my mother, it's the secrets and lies I was fed that kept me doubting myself. For five years, I watched the life being drawn from my mother's body while being constantly told she'd be fine. It made me question what I could clearly see with my own eyes. And the way I often handled it was by shutting down and removing myself from my feelings.

Today, they call it disassociation, but in 1961, we had no choice. Children's feelings were neither heard nor acknowledged— at least mine were not. And the thing that remains is PTSD, and this is what it looks like to me. Living alone can feel like social isolation and stir up feelings of loss. I worry that people I love will unexpectedly die. I fear the worst because I'm programmed not to trust what I see. Sometimes, it tricks me into thinking I'll end up totally alone and abandoned.

I was in therapy for more than ten years, and then I became a therapist. It was an opportunity to learn more about childhood trauma and also a way to help others. I became a Grief Therapist so that those suffering a loss could voice their despair in a safe place. It was my mission to accept their feelings without judgment so they could learn to eventually do that for themselves. Working with trauma helped me grow and become a more authentic person.

As the years have passed, I have also become resilient. And a big part of resilience is developing gratitude. I am grateful that my children have both turned out to be loving, well-adjusted people, with successful careers and wonderful spouses. They are all remarkable parents to my seven beautiful grandchildren.

I am also grateful that I lived this long life in excellent health. I have learned how to sift the truth from lies. I have good friends, community, and an abundance of love in my life. And every day I make a conscious decision to put gratitude and love before fear of loss. And that, I hope, will be my legacy.

The Scar

You can't reach my age without having scars. Suffering is part of the human condition, a familiar companion that I've learned to accept.

It was June of 1980, and I was seven months pregnant. I dropped my son off at daycare when a teacher pulled me aside. "I think you have blood on the back of your pants," she whispered. I ran to the bathroom, called my doctor, and went straight to the hospital.

After being poked and prodded, the doctor finally appeared. "It looks like the placenta is covering part of your cervix," he said. "If the baby delivers naturally… you could both bleed to death." I looked at him in disbelief as the tears welled up in my eyes.

"Don't worry," he said, trying to reassure me, "You'll probably be fine. The worst that will happen is you'll lose the baby." I opened my mouth, but he continued, "The closer it gets to term, the better your chances."

When my husband arrived, the nurse gave us instructions. "Complete bed rest to avoid further bleeding," she said. "But if it starts again, come right to the hospital, and we'll do a C-section."

Sydell and Emily, 2007

I caught my breath, and we made our way home. We hired a nanny to help us out, and I followed the doctor's orders. My due date was still eight weeks away, so I stayed in bed. I made it for almost two weeks. And then, I started to hemorrhage.

We took my son to a neighbor's and drove to the hospital. As soon as I got in the car, I started shivering. It felt like I was lost in a snowstorm and would never again be safe. I was still shaking when I got to the hospital, but they were expecting me. I was whisked away to the operating room and immediately prepped for surgery.

I was given a local anesthetic, and my body went numb. I felt a smooth blade move slowly across my abdomen. I heard soft voices all around me. I saw a doctor hand a tiny purple baby to the pediatrician.

And the room went still.

After a long silence, I started to panic. "What's the matter with my baby?" But nobody answered. The seconds were ticking away. And then, in the corner of the room, I heard it -- a faint cry that gradually gathered steam. The nurse grabbed my hand. "See, your baby's going to be fine," she said. "Oh, and it's a girl!"

We named her Emily. She was 5 pounds 6 ounces, and after a week in an incubator with tubes everywhere, I got to bring her home. And she thrived!

I have a beautiful scar where my daughter was born. I wear it with pride because she's filled my life with love. What a joy it's been to watch her grow up and have children of her own.

Suffering may be part of the human condition, but fortunately, so is JOY. And that's what keeps us alive… and coming back for more.

Role Reversal

It was 1985, and I kissed my daughter on her forehead. I call it her "keppe," the place where my lips could feel if she had a fever. Fortunately, her keppe was cool because this was the day of her surgery.

Emily was born with strabismus, commonly known as a lazy eye. We tried patches, bifocals, and many specialists, but after five years the decision was made. It was time to operate.

When they began prepping her for surgery, she became hysterical. I tried everything, but nothing would calm her down. Then I remembered the one thing that always works—BRIBERY.

I promised her not one, but two Cabbage Patch dolls. To me, they were the ugliest thing on the planet. But they were all the rage at the time, and it did the trick. She finally settled down, and they took her in.

Sydell & Emily 1982

Waiting was torture. My mind kept going to the worst-case scenario: they're going to cut the wrong muscle, and she'll be blind for the rest of her life. Or what if the anesthesia is too much, and she doesn't wake up?

After two hours, she was wheeled into recovery. The doctor told us everything went well. But when I saw blood dripping from her eyes, all I could think of was Oedipus Rex blinding himself with a spear.

The nurse reassured me that the bleeding was normal. And since it was my place to keep her calm, instead of reacting, I kissed her beautiful face and

Emily and Sydell 2022

brought her home.

Fast forward 38 years. My daughter is driving, and I'm in the passenger seat. We are on our way to Cedars Sinai for my knee replacement surgery. When we get to the 7th floor, we check-in. And before they take me away, Emily brings her lips to my forehead and kisses my keppe for luck.

Three hours pass in the blink of an eye while the surgery proceeds as planned. When it's over, and I'm in recovery, I slowly open my eyes. I'm calmed by the sight of my daughter, the one with the beautiful, straight eyes.

When did our roles get reversed? When did my daughter become the one in the driver's seat? I know it's the cycle of life, I just didn't think it would be here so fast. But this I do know for sure. No matter what happens in life, I will never be bribed into surgery…by the promise of a cabbage patch doll.

Make Your Life a Blessing

My 44-year-old son, Jason, is committed to living a meaningful life. He epitomizes the prayer: "Help us find the courage, to make our lives a blessing." And as senior rabbi of Cedars-Sinai, he has ample opportunity. Every day, he brings comfort and kindness to those in need of healing.

Jason manages the department of spiritual care, which includes over 40 chaplains of different religions. But his reach extends into the community, where he addresses subjects of interest, most recently the issue of artificial intelligence. He particularly enjoys bringing groups to the hospital for seminars or hands-on training. And because he has a PhD in medical ethics, he serves on ethics committees in and out of Cedars.

Unlike his talkative mother, Jason has a soft-spoken, compassionate nature. He can give a sermon like the best of them, but he is an introvert – more comfortable listening than he is speaking. In a recent article he was described as "the calm, unanxious presence amid everyday medical crises." And that is why he is so beloved.

Trust me: as a kid, he hid in the bushes after ringing neighbors' doorbells. He accidentally hit baseballs through their windows and rammed toy trucks into my walls. But at age 19, he made the decision to be a force of good in the world. And one of the ways he does it is through "mitzvot," acts of kindness both big and small.

So, before you think I am blowing hot air, I have one more thing to tell you. And it's a secret.

Jason is donating a kidney.

To a stranger

In Toronto

This Friday

Because it's a mitzvah. My son is a man who walks the talk. He is making his life a blessing, and I get to watch it all play out!

Jason, 2021

Toronto with Lauren

I wanted to move close to my son's family, but my daughter had her doubts.

"Mom," she began, "It's not going to work. You won't be happy living near Jason and Lauren."

"Why? What's the problem?"

"Jason has about 20 jobs, and Lauren's busy too. Don't expect to be friends."

"Em, don't worry, I'll work it out," I said, hoping she was wrong.

Despite her warning, I sold my house in Palos Verdes and found a cute house to rent in Beverly Hills.

Fast forward four years to 2023. Jason's about to fly to Toronto to donate a kidney. Lauren is planning on going, too, but she's nervous about leaving their 3-year-old daughter behind. My phone rings, and it's Jason.

**At the airport with Noa, Sydell, and Lauren.
February 2023**

"Mom, Lauren wants to bring Noa to Toronto, but only if you can come take care of her. I know it's a lot to ask, but you're one of the few people she trusts."

Even though I was nervous about his decision to donate a kidney, I was thrilled to be included. "I'd love to!" I answered. And the plans were finalized.

Jason flew to Toronto early for tests. Two days later, Lauren and I flew in. We worked together to manage the luggage, get through customs, and make sure that Noa was taken care of. Jason picked us up, and we all went back to the hotel.

I've always let Lauren take first place in Jason's life because she is his wife. And we all agreed it was better for me to stay at the hotel with Noa while Lauren took Jason to the hospital on the morning of his surgery. Since it was only two blocks away, Lauren could come back and forth with updates.

The day of the transplant arrived. At 6 a.m., Jason called my hotel room. "Lauren and I are ready to leave, and Noa's sleeping. Can you come to our room?" I threw a coat over my nightgown and walked two doors down the hall. Lauren was relieved, and I was happy to crawl into bed with Noa and go back to sleep.

When Lauren came back from the hospital, she told me about meeting the recipient's family and how they hugged her with love and gratitude. I was so touched by the story and her deep devotion to my son. And then I understood: Jason may get the accolades, but Lauren's the one who holds their lives together.

Lauren in 2018

It was good to feel needed on that trip and be an intimate part of their family. When two women love the same man, there's bound to be jealousy. But once your son gets married, his wife becomes the leading lady. And if you behave, you get to be a supporting player. It's the secret to having a good relationship with your daughter-in-law. We are all back home, and Jason's is as good as new. But something unexpected happened on that trip. Something that proved my daughter wrong. Jason may have donated a kidney, but Lauren and I became friends.

Zayde

It's bedtime for four-year-old Noa, and mommy and daddy are out. After I help her into pajamas and she brushes her teeth, she jumps onto her parents' bed. In comes ten-year-old Ely, who plops himself in between us. It's time to play "Best and Worst," our favorite game.

"O.K. Ely," I say, "What was the best part of your day?" He loves to go first and is quick to respond. "The best was playing baseball. And I made it to second base." "Oh, good for you!" I say. "Noa, what was the best part of your day?" She thinks for a minute until a light goes on in her head. "When YOU came over, grandma!" I laugh. This child is such a delight.

"Now, what was the worst part of your day, Ely?" He looks me in the eye. "When I got home from camp," he says as he catches his breath, "and Mommy was crying." Noa looks up. "Me too," she whispers. "The worst part of my day was when I heard that her daddy died."

We all get quiet, and when she's ready, Noa continues. "Where did he go, grandma? Will I ever see him again?" Those are big questions, and I want to answer in a way that supports their religious beliefs. "He's with God now," I begin, but Ely comes to my rescue. "He's with Hashem, Noa, and Hashem is everywhere, all around us."

When 14-year-old Ayden overhears, she joins us on the bed. "Hashem is in our hearts too, Noa, and his love is taking care of Zayde." Noa smiles and gets under the covers with Ayden and Ely. I gently rub Noa's back, which is part

Sydell's maternal grandparents: 1940 Edith Garlick Kay and Abraham Kay

Sydell's paternal grandparents: 1945 Laura Austin Horowitz and William (Vel Vel) Horowitz

of our bedtime routine. But just before she dozes off, her head pops up. "Am I going to die, grandma?" "Not for a really, really long time," I answer. She starts to relax, and before long, is fast asleep.

Although we're all sad about Zayde's death, the four of us are together on mommy and daddy's bed. What could be more precious than snuggling with loved ones and sharing a moment of deep sadness? I wonder why this was not part of my own childhood, although there were plenty of occasions.

Nonetheless, I am grateful to be sharing theirs, and experience what it means to be part of a loving family.

Knee Replacement Surgery

I was scared, but a nice man helped me out of bed.

He gave me a walker and we went down the hall.

Next morning my daughter came to bring me home.

"You have how many stairs in front of your house?"

I told the nurse, "Six," under my breath.

"We'll We'll test you on stairs before you're discharged."

I was scared, but I held tight to the railing.

I tried the first step and started to fall.

Em caught me on one side the nurse on the other.

"If you can't do the stairs you'll go home in a gurney."

"What about crutches," Emily asked.

The nurse found crutches, and I made it to the top.

Emily called Lauren who met us at home.

I was scared when I got there, but the girls helped me up.

I was relieved, I got better, still afraid I would fall.

I stayed home, I read, I watched dumb T.V.

A friend said she'd take me to class the next week.

I was glad to get out, and tried to be fine.

I was scared the next month when I returned to Plato.

I drove myself there, and the group inspired me.

I emailed Dianne, the Chair of Curriculum.

We were friends in class before the pandemic.

"Write a proposal and I'll give you some feedback."

I send her an outline for a class on Grieving.

I was scared as I waited for her to respond.

"I love it," she wrote. "and you'll be in charge."

It helped me remember who I used to be.

Before surgery made me feel weak and afraid.

It's three months later, I'm back on my feet.

The clouds are clearing and I'm ready to fly.

Sydell 2022 the Wallis Theatre

Connection

Is there anything more wondrous than human connection? To be seen, heard, and accepted for who we are is so precious. But like many of us post-pandemic, I've learned to feel safe in my own isolation.

On October 7th, shook by the news of Israel under attack, I knew I needed community. The next day was Simchat Torah, a holiday I rarely celebrated, but I got myself dressed and went to synagogue. The service was outside, so when I reached the seating area, I looked around. I was hoping to find someone who needed to connect as much as I did. I saw a woman sitting alone, so I walked over and sat next to her.

"Hi, I'm Sharon," she immediately said.

"I'm Sydell," I answered. "Do you have family in Israel?"

"Yes," she said. "My brother and his entire family live there. How about you?"

"My 19-year-old granddaughter is in Jerusalem and I'm worried sick. Have you spoken to your brother?"

We had a lot in common, and it was a release for us both.

The rabbi was very emotional and asked us to join him up front. I have a bad knee and was reluctant to get up, but Sharon gently led the way. Before I knew it, we were drawn into the circle, dancing around the Torah. We were all singing, "*Am Yisroel Chai*," an anthem of solidarity meaning, "the people of Israel live!" I eventually stepped aside to rest my knee, and like sunshine bursting through the clouds, Sharon came over to check on me.

When we returned to our seats, the conversation continued. We were both retired and living alone. Her brother was Orthodox, so I told her about my son. Like me, she was a new member and didn't come regularly. After services, we exchanged numbers and promised to stay in touch.

Two weeks later, there was a Shabbat dinner at temple. I normally skipped those events to avoid sitting alone. But instead, I texted Sharon. "Do you want to go to dinner at Beth Am this Friday?" I asked. She answered immediately.

"I was just deciding. Yes, let's sit together."

The evening was beautiful, and we enjoyed celebrating the culture we loved. But our connection is what made the difference. It helped me feel comfortable enough to show up in the first place. And then it came to me: belonging to the Jewish community meant I'd never have to feel alone. *Am Yisroel Chai*, the people of Israel live!

We Go On

It was an outdoor concert for peace and love, where hundreds of young people gathered. Suddenly, there was gunfire. People were screaming and running. Terrorists were chasing them down as their young bodies fell to the ground.

A few miles away, women were being pulled from their homes to be raped and tortured. Babies were burned alive, and children beheaded in front of their horrified parents. Survivors were dragged through an underground network of tunnels and taken hostage. These were tunnels built with money to "Free Palestine."

Since that day, I have observed four Jewish holidays. All of them are about enemies trying to destroy us. On Chanukah, we celebrate the miracle of eternal light. The oil supply was depleted because the Jews were under siege by the Greek-Syrian army.

On Purim, we applaud the bravery of Queen Esther. The King, influenced by Haman, was about to kill all the Jews in Persia. He listened to Queen

Esther and her Uncle Mordecai, who saved the Jews from annihilation.

On Passover, we retell the story of the Jews being slaves in Egypt. Each time Pharaoh agreed to release them, he reneged on his promise. The cry, "Let My People Go," comes from that time. The slaves finally made their exodus, only to wander the desert for the next 40 years.

Last week was Yom HaShoah, Holocaust Remembrance Day. We commemorated the murder of six million Jews by Nazi Germany. Vulnerable civilians – women, children, the elderly – were stripped naked and sent to the gas chambers, where they suffered horrific deaths.

And now we have Hamas, whose stated goal is the eradication of Israel. They rejected a two-state solution because they want the entire country "from the river to the sea." On October 7th, they violently attacked civilians, knowing full well that Israel would have to retaliate. They also knew retaliation would be condemned by the rest of the world… a win-win for Hamas.

So the question I'm asking is, WHY? In every generation, enemies try to destroy us. Why? How do we face Jew-hatred and still go on? We have to fight back. Because Never Again… is NOW.

A Place in the Sun

Mine was a life in the theatre. I never performed on Broadway or graced the silver screen. That wasn't important to me. What mattered was being able to express myself in a way that reached others. And more than that, I wanted to find a place to belong.

At 15, I played Yum Yum in Gilbert and Sullivan's *Mikado*. It was a camp play, but there were 500 in the audience. Alone on stage, I was hit by a spotlight… and I began to sing. It wasn't an operatic voice, but it was ON pitch, and I felt the audience with me. That's when I knew I was on the right track.

Performance in L.A., 1973

My freshman year of college, I auditioned for *The Fantasticks*. I had just seen Liza Minnelli play Louisa, so I knew the show well. As luck would have it, I got the part. Doing this play helped me go deeper and find the meaning behind the words. My favorite speech was El Gallo's, at the start of Act Two: "The play's not done/oh no, not quite/For life never ends in the moonlit night/ And despite what pretty poets say/ the night is only half the day/For the story is not ended/and the play never done/until we've all of us been burned a bit/and burnished by the sun."

As much as I loved performing, it was just the prelude. Directing taught me to look beyond myself and see the bigger picture. Before becoming a college professor, I paid my dues teaching high school drama. My students were doubtful when I gave them Paul Sills' *Story Theatre*. But when opening night came, and they stormed the stage singing, "Here Comes the Sun," I knew they were convinced. Performing brought them together and gave them a needed lesson in trust.

The real fun began when I directed university theatre. I had many students of color who were first in their families to go to college. But what they lacked in experience, they made up for in passion. We did color-blind casting in the 1980s before it became a fad. They tackled

Sydell with cast of The Importance of Being Earnest, 1990

Shakespeare, Oscar Wilde, Tennessee Williams, and more. And once they had the tools to interpret a text, they learned to speak with clarity and listen with intent.

Because here's the thing about theatre: you can't do it alone. You need designers and technicians, not to mention the cast, crew, and directors. And when everyone contributes to the same creative project, they develop deep personal connections. Is it any wonder that the rehearsal process was my favorite part of directing?

So when friends ask me if any of my students became famous, I smile politely and say, "To tell you the truth… that wasn't our mission."

My life in the theatre was much richer than fame and fortune. Year after year, I watched students discover that working together was the way to belong. When they traded in "lost and troubled" for "confident and poised," they took their place in the sun.

And guess what… So did I.

Sydell with cast & crew of Uncommon Women and Others, 1984

96

Hope for the Future

The ocean gives me hope. The waves have a rhythm that feel like an eternal heartbeat: pulsing and unbroken. When one is spent, washed up on the sand, another is right behind it. It reaches its own height and then settles down on the shore. The waves have order. They're predictable and feel like they will never end.

Not like the world today. Anger and hatred fill our airwaves. It's on TV and social media, and even on the streets, as people move away from each other if they get too close. It doesn't feel safe, this world we are inhabiting, and it makes it hard for me to believe that goodness will rule the day.

And I'm home way too much. I miss the oceans of the South Bay. The first year Rex and I were married, we'd go to the bluffs in Lunada Bay and climb our way down. We'd look out at the waves and believe in a future of hope.

The water has to bring me back because I can't stay in the fear. It's work for me, and it takes courage, but it's the only choice I have.

Tomorrow, I will go to the ocean and look out at the waves. And remember how you loved me, Rex, and try to be strong. I will try to bring the rhythm of waves to a quiet place within. So I can find hope for today and the future ahead.

Emily & Eric and kids 2023

And when my days are through, and it's time for me to leave this heavy earth, I will see myself as one of the waves. A wave which has run its course and come to rest on the shore. My rhythm will be done, but there will be more waves behind me. Waves of those I've birthed, and touched, and loved, that have yet to run their course.

Lauren & Jason and kids 2024

It is the order of things, and it's as it should be. Nobody lives forever – no lover, no parent, no idea, and no president. Life will go on, and even if I'm not here, I have faith that it will be good.

Made in the USA
Las Vegas, NV
05 November 2024

6e508a0a-e937-43c8-b2a3-70dbf835c588R01